Slave Ship *Guerrero*

The Wrecking of a Spanish Slaver off the coast of Key Largo, Florida with 561 Africans imprisoned in the hold while being pursued by the British warship HBM <u>Nimble</u> in 1827

Gail Swanson

ISBN 0-7414-2765-6

Cover Art by Renee Anderson, Marathon, Fla.

Published by:

INFIN ITY
PUBLISHING.COM

1094 New DeHaven Street, Suite 100
West Conshohocken, PA 19428-2713
Info@buybooksontheweb.com
www.buybooksontheweb.com
Toll-free (877) BUY BOOK
Local Phone (610) 941-9999
Fax (610) 941-9959

Printed in the United States of America
Printed on Recycled Paper
Published September 2005

Also by the Author:

*Documentation of the Indians of
the Florida Keys & Miami, 1513-1765*
(Infinity Publishing, 2003)

Acknowledgments

My thanks to those who gave great attention and favors that added significantly to the research, content, and production of this work: John Weiss in London, Betty Shannon in Barbados, J. G. "Jerry" Braddock Jr. and Pat Spaulding, both of Charleston, Russell Dwayne Ross and Babbs Ross Chittenden, both of Texas, Charles Carroll Keeler and Carol W. Kimball, both of Mystic, Ct., Dr. Patricia Griffin of St. Augustine, Dr. Brien Laing of Fernandina Beach, Fla., Roger Clark of the Kingsely Plantation, Dinizulu Gene Tinnie and Dr. William M. Straight, both of Miami, Renee Anderson of the Florida Keys, and especially, Sally Bishop, of the Florida Keys and now of Sebring, Fla., who cheerfully cared for and took command of the troops during my many explorations from Ft. Spring Lake.

Also, special documents were given to me by historians Jerry Wilkinson, Tom Hambright, and Jim Clupper, all of the Florida Keys.

Thank you, thank you, thank you - you've enriched this work tremendously.

Gail Swanson
July, 2005

For Andrea Cordani

of London,

With Thanks

This book is written in the memory of those Africans in the hold of the slave ship Guerrero. Of most of them there is no record of their subsequent lives enslaved in Cuba. For those who remained in US territory and survived to reach Liberia, West Africa, in 1830 there is. Their American-given names are:

Bartow, George, died 1841, Liberia
Bartow, Joseph, died 1839, Liberia
Brown, Andrew
Brown, Joseph
Clark, James
Clark, Thomas, died 1841, Liberia
Curtis, John
Dana, Joseph
Davis, Charles
Davis, David
Davis, Henry
Davis, Isaac, died 1838, Liberia
Davis, John
Davis, July
Davis, Thomas
Dawn, Friday, died 1842, Liberia
Dawn, Sampson, died 1837, Liberia
Devany, Henry
Devany, James
Devany, Samuel
Dozier, Munday
Fernandez, John, died 1838, Liberia
George, Lewis
George, Richard, died 1841, Liberia

Gibbs, Joseph
Gould, John
Hanson, Captain
Hanson, Chap, died 1840, Liberia
Hanson, John
Hanson, Peter
Jackson, Francis
Jeff, Joseph, died 1838, Liberia
John, Richard, died 1836, Liberia
Jones, Morice, died 1833, Liberia
Kinsley, Adam, died 1833, Liberia
Kinsley, David, died 1836, Liberia
Kinsley, Henry
Kinsley, James
Kinsley, Loumon, left Liberia for Sierra Leone in 1839
Kinsley, Marshall, died 1839, Liberia
Kinsley, Moses
Kinsley, Peter
Kinsley, Thomas
Kinsley, William
Kinsley, William (two men with the same name)
Kinsley, York
Kissey, George
Lewis, Emanuel, died 1837, Liberia
Lewis, Fernando
Lewis, John
Lewis, Joseph
Lewis, Robert, died 1841, Liberia
Lewis, Sampson
Lewis, Samuel
Lewis, Thomas
McGill, George
Moore, John, died 1836, Liberia
Paul, Augustus, died 1838, Liberia
Paul, Henry
Paul, John

Paul, Samuel
Russwurm, Caesar
Smith, Adam, died 1836, Liberia
Smith, Alexander, left Liberia for Gambia in 1833
Smith, Anthony
Smith, Archibald, died 1839, Liberia
Smith, George, died 1841, Liberia
Smith, Glasgow
Smith, Grudging, died 1830, Liberia
Smith, James
Smith, Jesse
Smith, John, died 1838, Liberia
Smith, Joseph
Smith, Lamb, left Liberia for Sierra Leone in 1839
Smith, Lewis
Smith, Major, died 1843, Liberia
Smith, Ned, died 1830, Liberia
Smith, Pedro
Smith, Pepper
Smith, Richard, died 1840, Liberia
Smith, Robert, died 1840, Liberia
Smith, Samuel
Smith, Thomas
Smith, Thomas (two men with the same name)
Stewart, Douglass, died 1839, Liberia
Stewart, John
Stone, John
Travis, Cyrus
Travis, Philip
Tucker, Philip
Williams, Henry, died 1837, Liberia[1]
John[2]

Table of Contents

Introduction: A Journey into Records of Forgotten People

i

Chapters
1. *July, 1827 Havana, Cuba*
   The Slave Ship *Guerrero* Sails

   1

2. *Fall, 1827 Africa*
   Man's Inhumanity to Man: Slavery

   5

3. *December, 1827 Waters off Orange Cay, Bahamas, to the Florida Reef*
   The British Warship's Chase and the Wrecking of the *Guerrero*

   12

4. *December, 1827 Carysfort Reef off Key Largo, Florida Keys*
   Rescue by Americans - then Brazen Action by the Slave Traders

   17

5. *December, 1827 Carysfort Reef and Santa Cruz*
   Second Hijacking to Cuba

   23

6. *December, 1827 Carysfort Reef*
   Armed: Fearing Another Hijacking

   29

7. *December, 1827 - March, 1828 Key West, Florida*
   Fear & Legal Arguments at an Island Village

   33

8. January, 1828 Havana
   Evading Spain's Law: 398 Lost to Slavery
                                                    46

9. January, 1828 Charleston, South Carolina
   The Wreckers' Plea for Payment
                                                    49

10. 1828 – 1829 Northeast Florida
    Plantation Slavery
                                                    57

11. Washington, D. C. 1828 - 1829
    Inadequate Response in the Capital
                                                    66

12. September, 1829 Amelia Island, Florida
    Return to Africa
                                                    75

13. December, 1829 Carlisle Bay, Barbados
    In Terrible Distress
                                                    94

14. May & June, 1831 St. Augustine, Washington,
    Norfolk
    John, the Last African
                                                    101

15. 1830 – 1843 Liberia
    Records of the Africans' Lives in Liberia
                                                    105

Epilogues .
                                                    123

Appendixes
    Before Becoming Human Cargo
                                                    132

    Log of HBM *Nimble* December 19, 1827
                                                    139

    Thoughts on Location of the Shipwreck
                                                    141

Key West of the 1820s: The Lion's Mouth

149

Africans & African-Americans at Key West
  1821 - 1833: Events at a Little Island

154

Biographical Material

161

Discussion on Identity of the Africans

177

Chronological List of Documents

180

Bounty List, HBM *Nimble*

192

Partial List of the Crew of the *Guerrero*

195

Accounting of the 561 People in the *Guerrero*

197

Endnotes and Index

"In 1827, one hundred and twenty-five vessels sailed from Cuba to Africa, for Slaves."

American Colonization Society, 1830[3]

The slave trade was "the most demoniac pursuit which the spirit of avarice ever prompted fallen man to engage in."

American Colonization Society, 1838[4]

"Of the nature of this traffic...It begins in corruption, and plunder, and kidnapping. It creates and stimulates unholy wars, for the purpose of making captives. It desolates whole villages and provinces, for the purpose of seizing the young, the feeble, the defenceless, and the innocent. It breaks down all the ties of parent, and children, and family, and country. It shuts up all sympathy for human suffering and sorrows. It manacles the inoffensive females, and the starving infants. It forces the brave to untimely death, in defence of their humble homes and firesides; or drives them to despair and self-immolation. It stirs up the worst passions of the human soul, darkening the spirit of revenge, sharpening the greediness of avarice, brutalizing the selfish, envenoming the cruel, famishing the weak, and crushing to death the broken-hearted. This is but the beginning of the evils. Before the unhappy captives arrive at the destined market, where the traffick ends, one quarter part at least, in the ordinary course of events, perish in cold blood, under the inhuman or thoughtless treatment of their oppressors.

Strong as these expressions may seem, and dark as is the colouring of this statement, it is short of the real calamities inflicted by this traffick. All the wars that have isolated Africa for the last three centuries, have had their origin in the slave-trade. The blood of thousands of her miserable children has stained her shores, or quenched the dying embers of her desolated towns, to glut the appetite of slave dealers. The ocean has received in its deep and silent bosom thousands more, who have perished from disease and want, during their passage from their native homes to the foreign colonies. I speak not from vague rumours, or idle tales, but from authentic documents, and the known historical details of the traffick - a traffick that carries away at least fifty thousand[5] persons annually, from their homes and their families, and breaks the hearts, and buries the hopes, and extinguishes the happiness of more than double that number. There is...something of horror in it, that surpasses all the bounds of the human imagination."

A Few Facts Respecting the American Colonization Society, and the Colony at Liberia
pamphlet, American Colonization Society (1830)

Introduction:

A Journey into Records of Forgotten People

In 1990 I began a study of Florida Keys history for the period before the American settlement (which began in 1822) of America's tropical archipelago. I was not a historian, I was a naturalist, and had by then lived on the Keys for 10 years. In finishing my first work, "A Calendar of the Florida Keys" I did some intense library work on Keys nature, involving a long six-hour round trip every few weeks for a year up to the downtown Miami library, the local libraries having almost nothing on my subject.

My calendar was a day by day record of fish migrations, bird migrations, native plant bloom times, and every recorded periodical event of the lives of the crabs, snakes, turtles, deer, coral, insects, etc. of the Keys and their waters.

I finally had about 300 entries for my calendar of the Keys. But I needed 365. I decided to plug the empty days with historical events at the Keys. What I needed was a lot of dates, then I could move the birds and blooms over a day or so around them with no loss of correctness. And I found a book with a lot of dates: Robert Marx' *Shipwrecks in Florida Waters*. So then I started going the opposite direction for library work, the 60 miles from my Middle Keys home to Key West, to the Monroe County Public Library local history room.

There I found little on the Keys shipwrecks Robert Marx wrote of, and eventually became aware why: many of them occurred in the pre-American period of Keys history, for Marx obviously had done a great deal of his research in Spain and England, not the United States. The events of three centuries (1500s, 1600s, and 1700s) at the Keys could not be found in the Key West library history room. To make a long story shorter, I appointed myself as the discoverer of the "forgotten three centuries" of Keys history and decided to give a year of my life to the project. That was 15 years ago and I'm still working on it - the richest, most diverse history of anywhere in the entire Western Hemisphere.

For my project I hired a researcher familiar with the Public Record Office in London, Andrea Cordani, to obtain logs of British warships that had wrecked at the Keys during the time period I was studying. Andrea was not only efficient and highly knowledgeable but also seemed to know that I was seeking information on people who weren't much in Florida - or any other - history books.

One day at a Keys library where I donated copies of all my discoveries, Monroe County Public Library at Islamorada, Jim Clupper, the head librarian, showed me four pages from a book entitled *The Territorial Papers of the United States, Florida* (Clarence Edwin Carter, compiler). The pages were of two documents about a slave ship and a British warship, HBM (His Britannic Majesty's) *Nimble* 100 miles from Key West. Jim thought I should get that ship's log in London copied too. And I thought he should go jump in a lake since the documents were dated 1827 - in the American period of the Keys - and I was studying the *pre-American* history of the Keys.

But no one I knew of had copied the log of that warship from the archives before and I doubted any Keys historian ever would, for besides Robert Marx I am one of only two historians (Jack Haskins the other) to comb records located in Great Britain for Keys history. And there was an exact date in that book, so if the log was extant I wouldn't have to pay Andrea for much time to search through it. So, mostly to avoid guilt feelings that would come from *not* doing it, I asked Andrea to look for the log.

The log was extant, but one of the log pages I received was written in such small handwriting I could hardly read it. I didn't even take time to try to transcribe it, just filed it away and went on with my regular work. But I did note that it recorded a sea fight off the Upper Keys, at Carysfort Reef.

Six months later I was in a New Orleans library researching French ships that had been at the Keys in the 1700s. While heading down the stacks at a fast pace - for I had a hotel bill running - my eye caught on a title on American history in British archives. I forced myself to stop with the French for five minutes and look through the book.

In it were many references to HBM *Nimble* at Key West, and the references were to Foreign Office papers at the Public Record Office. Andrea and I had been working in the Admiralty papers for maritime events, and I wondered why the Foreign Office (the equivalent of our State Department) would be involved in little Key West. Curiosity dragged me out of my favorite three centuries to a fourth one, the 1800s.

When I got back home I mailed the references to Andrea.

I got a call from London. So many papers here, she told me with her elegant British accent, on a Spanish slave ship and HBM *Nimble* and the Key Westers that I couldn't possibly afford to have them all copied. But Andrea Cordani had an alternate plan, and she sat in the Public Record Office reading all those papers for hours into a tape recorder. It took me months to transcribe it - months of hours daily listening to the records of an event that involved 561 hopeless Africans, some 90 ruthless Spaniards in the slave trade, scores of British Royal Navy men, and American seafarers. Later research in US archives added Indians of North Florida, southern plantation owners, the governor of Barbados, the people of the new settlement of Liberia, Africa, and even President John Quincy Adams, all involved in a true drama of humanity.

For at least a year after transcribing the tape from London I felt as if I had about 120 people with me all the time. They were the Africans saved from the slave ship that remained for awhile in US territory. I had found them in the archives and so I was responsible to them.

I went to Charleston and imagined the Key West wreckers walking the street to General Geddes' house, hoping for his help; to Savannah; to Mystic, Ct. in 1995 and 2003 trying to find something on a fisherman, Austin Packer, caught up in the horrible events; to St. Augustine and Gainesville and Amelia Island and Fort George Island, Fla.; to London in 2002 and to Washington in 2003 and 2004 tracking down more of their story. It has been 13 years of work but I felt it must be done, for the people in that slave ship had been totally forgotten.

At times I felt as if I could not write this book; that I didn't know enough about the slave trade. One of the books I referred to often was Hugh Thomas' *The Slave Trade: the story of the Atlantic slave trade, 1440-1870.* It had a daunting 908 pages. Another was *Report of Mr. Kennedy, of Maryland, from the Committee on Commerce of the House of Representatives of the United States on the African Slave Trade*, and it had 1,088 pages. Maybe I should just forget it. But I couldn't, because in all those pages of information there was only one paragraph on the people of the *Guerrero*.

(The only other current documentation besides those four pages in *The Territorial Papers* were short articles by North Florida historians that were wrong; one even with *fabricated* facts.)

The *Guerrero* was, after all, just one ship of *thousands* involved in the slave trade, the people aboard just a few hundred of *millions* transported. I had to learn about the horrors of the slave trade after I found records of the *Guerrero*. I hadn't found the *Guerrero* by studying the slave trade.

Hugh Thomas wrote this in his book:

It may be said that that [the history of the slave trade] is now such well-plowed ground that there is no room for any new cultivation...But any commercial undertaking involving the carriage of millions of people, stretching over several hundred years, involving every maritime European nation, every Atlantic-facing African people (and some others), and every country of the Americas, is a planet of its own, always with room for new observations, reflections, evidence...[6]

Those words furnished me with resolve to finish the traveling, the research, this book, because of that last word, *evidence*. Some day, perhaps, even the remains of the slave ship *Guerrero* will be found.[7]

I've found a lot in 13 years about the people who surrounded me in 1992, even how their lives were going in Liberia to 1843. Sixteen years before then they had been in the horrible hold of a slave ship bound to Cuba.

Chapter One

July, 1827
Havana, Cuba

The Slave Ship *Guerrero* Sails

The slave trade - the forced transportation of black Africans to the Western Hemisphere to be enslaved - had been banned 20 years before by British law, 19 years by US law, and seven years before by Spain. (The institution of slavery itself in the Western Hemisphere was beginning to be banned: the independent countries of Venezuela, Colombia and Chile had abolished slavery in 1821. In 1827, the year of this event, New York freed 10,000 enslaved people.) Yet the "trade" continued unabated to the Spanish colony of Cuba. The island's agricultural economy required many laborers, and the wealthy planters were determined to stay wealthy at the expense of the very lives of others. For the year 1827 British officials at Havana recorded 3,500 Africans landed from the holds of the slavers.

This is just one event of one of the most enormous crimes in human history: the African slave trade. It is estimated that 15 million Africans were transported across the Atlantic in conditions of horror, that at least 2 million more died in the slave ships.

Preserved in British archives in a modern building in London is a record of the beginning of what was one of the most dramatic events in the coastal maritime history of the United States:

Havannah, July 31, 1827

His Majesty's Commissioners to Mr.
[Foreign] Secretary [George] Canning [in
London][8]

Sir,

The illicit slave trade from this port, which
has been for some time on the decline,
appears to be about to resume its former
activity, no less than four Spanish vessels
having during the present month sailed for the
coast of Africa, and others being we
understand in a state of preparation. The
vessels which have sailed are the brigs
Guerrero and *Gallo* and the schooners
Lambery and *Indagadora*[9] of which Joze
Gomez, Ramon Gonzalez, Pedro Antonio
Salduondo, and Santiago Manzana, are
respectively the masters.

The *Guerrero* is an old slave-trader, and was
formerly called the *San Joze*. She is well
armed, and has a crew of ninety men; and
there can be little doubt that her purpose is to
plunder of their cargoes of slaves any weaker
vessels that she may fall in with on the coast
of Africa. This, we have heard, is a very
general practice of the Spanish slave vessels
fitted out at this port, which are almost all
well armed and manned.

Henry T. Kilbee
W. S. Macleay[10]

One of the writers of that letter, Irish lawyer Henry
Theo Kilbee wrote once that with very few exceptions, the
employees of the Cuban government were directly or

indirectly financially involved in the slave trade.[11]

In fact two years before, in 1825, the captain-general (governor) of the island, Francisco Dionisio Vives, wrote privately to his minister of foreign affairs that he concealed the existence of the slave trade because he was convinced that without slave labor "the island's wealth will disappear" for the culture of sugar cane and coffee depended upon slaves.[12]   The Cuban sugar plantations alone numbered nearly 1,000 in 1827, with an average of 70 enslaved people on each plantation.[13]

Between 1822 and 1829 British commissioners in Havana reported 152 completed slave ship voyages (all banned under Spanish law) with 43,150 Africans landed. But those were only reports of the Havana area.   Scholar David Eltis, analyzing the trade to the entire island for the same period, calculates 64,159 Africans were landed.[14]

Great Britain had been at times in the 1700s the most dominant of nations in the Atlantic slave trade. (One evidence of that activity is the three known British slave ships wrecked at the Florida Keys.)[15]   But there had been social changes, and in the 1800s the British government then hunted those in the inhumane "trade." There was a British squadron off the coast of Africa to stop the slavers. But the British also had second nets around the primary destinations of those slave ships: Brazil and Cuba. An 1818 Anglo-Spanish treaty set up tribunals; one at Havana. It was called the Mixed Commission Court, and was to deal with both British and Spanish captured slave ships and their human cargoes. It was the captures made near Cuba by the British and Spanish navies that the Havana court would decide.

The makeup of the Court was seriously flawed, however. It called for one British judge, one Spanish judge (who was usually profiting from the slave trade), and two arbitrators, one British and one Spanish. If the judges could not decide the case one of the arbitrators would.   *Which* arbitrator was decided by a dice roll.[16]

The Court could not punish owners or captains or crews of the slavers, only decide the fate of the ship and of

3

the Africans it was bringing to Cuba. The operation of the court was why Commissioners Kilbee and William Sharp Macleay were in Havana.

The *Guerrero* (the name means "warrior") sailed from there for Africa on July 14th.[17]

It can be reconstructed[18] that Kilbee's and Macleay's information on the *Guerrero* and the other slave ships was also sent to Lt. Edward Holland, commanding the warship HBM (His Britannic Majesty's) *Nimble*, in the nearby Bahamas.

Chapter Two

Fall, 1827
Africa

Man's Inhumanity to Man: Slavery

What trials the Africans in the hold of the *Guerrero* had suffered are little known: the conditions of their capture, their forced travel; probably roped and yoked together in lines to the coast, their captivity in the slave pens or fortresses for probably weeks until their sale, and a pirate attack at sea.

They perhaps were captives of warring chiefs in the Nigeria area. E. C. Irving reconstructed in 1856 the events of a war 30 years before. In the *Church Missionary Intelligencer* he wrote:

> To the north-east of and near to Ibadan are the extensive ruins of Owu....With this city originated the civil war which reduced to ruins so many towns once large and prosperous....From Mr. Barber, native catechist at Ibadan...we derived much information. A native of Ijemo, he was taken captive at the destruction of that place, and followed his new master into Ijebu country. He was with the army which besieged Ikreku [Ikereku Idan]. The town, he states was destroyed in 1826, as it was the year previously to his being liberated at Sierra Leone, which he knows to have been 1827...
>
> [Note - Barber thus was recounting that he had been forced into slavery due to this war

5

and eventually freed probably from a slave ship by the British in 1827. Slavers captured off the African coast by British warships were taken to British Sierra Leone, West Africa.]

A quarrel...fell out between the two chief leaders of the army, Laboshinde and Maye....Laboshinde...went with the Ijebus....Maye went and settled in Iporo. From these separate places the two divisions of the army went out daily, kidnapping and destroying the smaller towns, the Ijebu slave-dealers always offering a ready market for their captives.[19]

The murderous league,
The bribe for blood, is struck

James Grahame, *Africa Delivered*[20]

A conversation between a chief and Colonel Nicholls at Fernando Po, quoted in an 1830 memorial, related a reason why the chiefs cooperated with the slave traders:

The chief...said that, when I was gone, the slavers would come, and if he did not get slaves for them they would burn his town, and perhaps take away himself and his family, in place of the slaves they expected him to collect for them; but if this could be prevented, he would sell no more slaves.[21]

In 1826 at the River Bonny, less than 100 miles to the west of Calabar on the Nigerian coast a Capt. Vidal observed "twelve sail of slavers."[22] A traveler, Macgregor Laird, noted that at least 28,000 captive Africans were laden on ships at this location in the 1827 to 1834 era.[23]

Exactly where the Africans were from is uncertain, for as the British commissioners in Havana suspected would happen, the *Guerrero* attacked other slave ships, and where they were laden probably can never be known.

Later Kilbee and Macleay wrote to London:

We understand that she carried her [piratical] intention fully into effect, and that she not only plundered slave vessels but some other merchant ships, and accordingly at the time of her capture and loss she had a valuable cargo of European merchandize on board.[24]

Colonel Nicholls wrote in the same 1830 memorial previously quoted, as to piracy:

The individuals engaged in this traffic are persons of the most infamous and unprincipled descriptions; they come in their ships to the mouths of the different unexplored rivers, where they land a quantity of trade goods of the worst kind, and, leaving their supercargoes to exchange them with the chiefs for slaves, return to the sea whilst their cargoes are collecting, where, as pirates, they rob our merchant ships, murder their crews, and when glutted with plunder, return to the coast to ship their victims for whom they pay about 7 or 8 pounds apiece, and sell them for 70, 80, or 100 pounds each.

Isaac Mayo, commander of the Key West-based USS *Grampus*, having captured a laden Spanish slaver preparing to rob an American merchant ship off Hispaniola in 1830 wrote: "We know that most piracies, recently committed, have been by vessels engaged in this [slave] trade."[25]

Historian W. E. F. Ward relates two cases of pirating slave cargoes in his book *The Royal Navy and the Slavers*. Two prizes (captured slavers) with British crews put aboard and enroute to Sierra Leone were subsequently captured from the British by a Spanish pirate and taken to Havana. Ward relates another event, the robbing of a human cargo aboard the *Maria* by a pirate that certainly could have been the *Guerrero*. The *Maria* had purchased her cargo via another slaver from Duke Ephraim (or Aphrom), a black slave trader at Calabar, coast of Nigeria. After she was robbed she turned pirate also, robbing a Brazilian vessel laden with people from the Congo River. The *Maria* was chased by British cruiser HBM *Skipjack* off the coast of Cuba in November, 1827, just weeks before the *Guerrero* returned from Africa, perhaps with *Maria*'s original human cargo in her hold.[26]

The size of the *Guerrero* is not known, but her armament and crew were indeed that of a pirate slave ship. She carried 14 cannon: 4 long brass 12 pounders, able to fire a 12 pound cannon ball, and 10 iron 12 pounders,[27] with 89 to 96[28] men.

With hundreds of people chained in the hellish hold the *Guerrero* sailed westward toward her destination.

> **The sails are reefed;**
> **All hatches closed; the coffined captives pant**
> **For air; and in their various languages**
> **Implore, unheard, that but a single board**
> **Be raised: vain prayer, for now the beetling**
>   **surge**
> **Breaks o'er the bow, and boils along the deck.**
> **Oh then the horrors of the den below!**
>   James Grahame, *Africa Delivered*

Perhaps some 700 people had been forced aboard the ship, considering the death rate for slaving voyages of 15 to 20 percent or more. There were 561 still alive, having survived the horrors of the hold, as the ship approached Cuba in December.

Witnesses to the condition of rescued Africans brought into Key West, Florida, decades later, in 1860, relate what they saw of the horror of a slave ship. M. H. Stacey, seaman aboard USS *Crusader* at Key West wrote to his father of the condition of the Africans, mostly children ages 12 to 16, aboard the American slave ship *Wildfire*:

> Well I have visited the slaves. It was a sight which those who have not seen can form no idea of whatsoever. It was disgusting to all the senses. In the first place your nose was offended at an infernal stench...upon ascending the side ladder we observed perhaps one hundred & fifty little black children lying about & standing around the great portion in a state of absolute nakedness....it was an horrible sight to see the poor creatures, in all stages of emaciation, make their appearance. A glance on the slave deck was enough to fill the mind with indescribeable horror at what the poor creatures must have suffered in twenty-eight days passage. The deck was constructed of rough unplaned planks and raised from the ship's bottom about three feet leaving a space of about four feet in height and extending fore and after, in this the little fellows were huddled together....It was altogether horrible beyond description.[29]

Commander of USS *Mohawk* Lt. T. Augustus Craven also wrote a description of the *Wildfire*, to convince the Secretary of the Navy that the Africans could not travel further than the first American port reached, which was Key West, for it was a capture of a slaver enroute to Cuba:

> The negroes are packed below in as dense a mass as it is possible for human beings to be crowded; the space allotted them being in general about 4' high...are obliged to attend the calls of nature in this place - tubs being provided for the purpose - and here they pass their days, their nights, amidst the most horribly offensive odors...under the scorching heat of the tropical sun, without room enough for sleep; with scarcely space to die in; with daily allowance of food and water barely sufficient to keep them alive.[30]

There was nothing unusual about the conditions aboard the slave ship *Wildfire* of 1860, 33 years after the *Guerrero* was laden with human beings. A slave ship was a slave ship. But if one feels need of a report nearer to the time of the *Guerrero*, there was one, by the reverend Robert Walsh, returning home aboard a naval vessel in 1829, HMS *North Star*, when the *Veloz* was intercepted:

> She had taken in, on the coast of Africa, 336 males and 226 females, making in all 562, and had been out seventeen days, during which she had thrown overboard 55. The slaves were all inclosed under grated hatchways between decks. The space was so low that they sat between each other's legs and [were] stowed so close together that there was no possibility of their lying down or at all changing their position by night or day.[31]

The same year, 1829, HBM *Monkey* captured the slaver *Midas* near Bimini, the Bahamas, enroute to Havana. The *Monkey*'s log keeper recorded, "Found many of the

10

negroes to be very ill & that they were dying very fast from small pox, diarrhea, & scurvy."[32]

In addition to enduring the conditions of the hold of the *Guerrero* - in chains - there was still more horror of the 4,000-mile-long voyage ahead for the captive Africans. It would happen off the tip of Florida.

Chapter Three

December, 1827
Waters off Orange Cay, Bahamas,
to the Florida Reef

The British Warship's Chase
and the Wrecking of the *Guerrero*

On December 17, 1827, the British warship HBM *Nimble* was cruising the Florida Straits to intercept slave ships enroute to nearby Cuba.

That day the British fired two shots at and boarded a Baltimore schooner, the *Lapwing*,[33] enroute to New Orleans, and at the same time shot at the *Reuben Ross*, enroute to Key West, also from Baltimore, which outran her.[34]

Two days later near Orange Cay, the Bahamas, another vessel was sighted. Apparently the *Guerrero* was sailing from the north down the Florida Straits in attempting to evade British warships patrolling the long northern coast of Cuba. The *Guerrero* had only 250 miles more to sail before reaching the coast near Havana. It was noon. From HBM *Nimble*'s log:

> Sail in sight...Observed stranger to be a suspicious looking brig. I set topsail, cleared for action & fired 2 guns to bring stranger to whom we observed hauling up to avoid us; made more sail.[35]

She was, the British may have thought, one of the slavers that had sailed from Havana for Africa in July. The pursuit was on. HBM *Nimble* carried officers, marines, and crew totaling 56,[36] had 8 "guns" (cannon)[37] according to one source but another states "two gunades and an 18 [pounder] on a pivot"[38] and measured 83'7" on her deck, 22'2" beam and 9'5" depth of hold.[39] Later written of her opponent the *Guerrero* was this:

> Her force was sufficient to have blown the *Nimble* out of water at one broadside - why the Captain...did not do so, may appear strange; but he says he depended upon his vessel's sailing...did not wish to risk the lives of his negroes, when he could escape by superior sailing...[40]

During the first five hours of chasing the *Guerrero* the weather turned bad from a cold front pushing through. In *Nimble*'s log:

> 5:00 Strong breezes and squally with a heavy swell, carrying a heavy press of sail & gaining on chase. Observed her bear up.
>
> 6:15 Having closed considerably fired a gun to bring her to which was returned immediately by her guns & musquetry. Commenced action.

The events were also later reported in a letter written from Key West, certainly from information given by a member of *Nimble*'s crew:

> A sail was reported ahead, to which chase was immediately given, and continued until dark, when she attempted to cross the *Nimble*'s bow, by bearing round up, when at a quarter past six she was brought to action, which was briskly kept up on both sides.

Dusk became night as the ships approached the Florida Reef. The *Guerrero* appeared to be sailing at the rate of ten miles an hour,[41] a very fast sailing ship for the time. Although most ships of the day had copper sheathing at the waterline to avoid drag from barnacles the *Guerrero* was coppered all the way to the bottom, hence her speed.[42]

Six miles off Key Largo there was a lightship - stationed by American government one year before, to warn mariners of a dangerous coral reef that parallels the Florida Keys archipelago. Aboard the lightship *Caesar* Capt. John Whalton could see the flash and hear the report of the guns.[43] The battle between the ships was going on about ten miles to the northeast of his lightship.

The hundreds jammed in the hold of the *Guerrero* could not have known what was going on above them, why the cannon fire, the gunfire.

After 30 minutes of the sea fight the captain of the *Guerrero* pretended to surrender to the British by showing a light. The *Nimble*'s log:

6:45 Ceased firing & hauled up after her...

But more went on than was recorded in the ship's log. The letter writer at Key West revealed a bluff by the Spaniards:

[The slave ship] having, about a quarter before seven, slackened her fire, she hauled to the wind, fired a blank cartridge, and showed a light to leeward, when the *Nimble* ceased firing. After having thus apparently struck [her flag, a sign of surrender] the chase made off, and after being again pursued, it was found the *Nimble* was in 6 fathoms [36'] water, off the Florida coast.[44]

The log:

6:45 Having regular soundings from 6 to 4 fathoms approaching Florida reef.

7:30 Observed chase on shore.

Not knowing where in the entire world they were, or what the ship hit, or why, scores in the hold perished in the *Guerrero*'s collision with the coral reef.[45] The slaver's hull tore open. Then the masts fell. There were about 650 people onboard when this happened, Spanish and African, their screams "appalling beyond description."[46] The crew of the *Nimble*, which was over two miles away, was probably the source of the following in the Bahamas newspaper:

> The masts of the chase were heard to fall with a tremendous crash, and a horrid yell from those onboard, which left no doubt of her being a Guineaman.[47]

Reacting to the danger, the British crew tried staying their schooner - trying to go about, to avoid hitting the reef.[48] Five minutes later, at 7:35, HBM *Nimble* also struck the coral.

The emotions of the British of the situation can only be imagined. The intended rescuers had chased a laden slave ship into dangerous waters and had heard the screams of the people they meant to rescue from a life of slavery cross two miles of ocean. In minutes or hours they could have no life at all.

An anchor was put out in the 4 fathom (24') deep water, the sails furled, ballast and shot were thrown overboard to lighten the warship, but in a half hour her movement in the swells broke the anchor line. HBM *Nimble* drove further onto the reef. Twenty minutes later, drifted off the reef into 2 fathoms (12'), another anchor was put out, but the warship drifted right back onto the reef. The tide receded. The *Nimble* moved no more. There could be no rescue. It was then about 9:00, and still squally.

President John Quincy Adams would become involved with the fate of many of the Africans aboard the *Guerrero*. At about that very time, in the evening of December 19, 1827, he was writing the day's events in his diary which coincidentally included: "a resolution asking for the correspondence with the British Government relating to the erection of lighthouses on the coast of Florida."

The lights of the lightship, apparently, had been too weak to warn where the dangerous reef was.[49]

On the wreck of the *Guerrero* 90 ruthless Spaniards in the slave trade and 561 helpless Africans were on a ship off an uninhabited coast six miles from land, in cold and stormy weather, at night, sinking. By morning the ship had turned over onto her side, and was full of water.[50] And 41 of the Africans, crushed by the movements of the bottoms of the masts, or drowned, were never seen again.

Chapter Four

December, 1827
Carysfort Reef off Key Largo, Florida Keys

Rescue by Americans -
then Brazen Action by the Slave Traders

Six years before, in 1821, the United States received Florida from Spain. The next year a little settlement formed on one of the Florida Keys nearest Havana: Key West. The island had fresh water ponds and a fine deep-water harbor. The economy of the 1 x 3 1/2 mile island was based on fishing for the Havana market - Havana only 90 miles away - and on "wrecking" - that is, saving ships that ran onto the reef, and/or their cargoes, for a portion of their value. Actually, for *most* of their value.

There had been shipwreck salvors at the Keys since the 1500s. The native Calusa-related Indians had worked the many wrecks, and after their evacuation in the 1760s to Cuba (due to the raids of the invading Creek-related tribes, today's Seminoles) the seafarers of the nearby Bahama Islands worked the wrecks, free of the fear of Indians, for the Creeks did not settle on the Keys. When the Keys became American territory, the "wreckers" were Americans. It was a prosperous business to be in for anyone, for there were always wrecks.

The waters of the Florida Keys are very dangerous for mariners. This area named the Straits of Florida is where the Gulf of Mexico flows into the lower-level Atlantic, creating a powerful current between Florida and Cuba that leads into the Gulf Stream, which provides a fast return sail to Europe. Sailing in this current has been the plan of every ship master leaving the Gulf of Mexico or western Caribbean since its speed and direction were discovered by Ponce de Leon's pilot in 1513.

The current caused the building of the perilous coral reefs offshore, bringing coral polyps to the continental shelf, with warm water, oxygen, and nutrients - and, at latitude 24, there was plenty of sunshine available. The result of the coral reef building over eons of time is what has been described as a "labyrinth."[51] The islets called the Keys (from the Spanish word *cayos*) are the remains of a dead, more ancient coral reef, now exposed due to changes in sea level. The jagged, submerged living rocks a few miles offshore have bilged ships of many nations, or held them stranded upon them.

An estimated 1,000 shipwrecks now lie off the Florida Keys. Among the reasons they are there are the reef, the current, with huge waves when winter fronts hit from the North American mainland, sudden eddies of the current towards shore, wars, pirate attacks, and frequent hurricanes.

On that night in December, 1827, anchored at Black Caesar's Creek in the Upper Florida Keys about 100 miles from Key West, its occupants hoping for a wreck, were the wreckers *Thorn*, Capt. Charles Grover, and the aptly-named *Surprize*, Capt. Samuel Sanderson. The *Thorn* had eight men aboard,[52] the number aboard the *Surprize* is unknown. The wreckers (a term used both for the vessels and for the men) saw the ships the next morning and Capt. Grover hastened to the scene, getting there by 6:00 a.m. Arriving first made him "wreck master" and in charge of operations. (It is not recorded that the men at Black Caesar's Creek heard the battle at sea, and with the direction of the wind during a usual cold front coming off the Florida mainland the sound may not have reached them.)

Grover came to the closest ship, the *Guerrero*. He launched a boat and with two men sailed for the warship, leaving orders to his mate to take possession of the slaver. When mate Nathaniel Glover came to the wreck in *Thorn's* other boat Capt. Joze Gomez told him to raise the American

18

flag over it, showing it was the prize of the Americans, and not of the British, who had been unable to board and take possession.

Upon reaching the grounded warship *Nimble*, Capt. Grover heard just the opposite - the vessel's captain, Lt. Holland, told Grover the ship he had just left was his, Holland's, prize. Holland's men were in the act of throwing over their large deck pivot gun when Grover arrived. Grover asked Lt. Holland "if he wished assistance who answered in the affirmative."[53] Then with a British officer and two seamen put aboard his boat Grover sailed to the *Surprize* then also at the scene and requested Capt. Sanderson to attend to the *Nimble*.

Although the priority of working the *Nimble* given to the *Surprize* seems lacking in humanity - for hundreds of people were clinging for life on the wreck of the slaver - it was probably done at the insistence of Lt. Holland who surely wanted to be in control of the situation but who wouldn't be until his ship was sailing again. But it also may have been a business decision on the part of Grover to give attention to the party that, he believed, would be paying his salvage fee; a salvage fee for pulling the warship off the coral and a salvage fee for saving who may have been thought briefly as "property" of the British - that is, the enslaved Africans. Three decades later in Key West history Judge William Marvin wrote in his *Treatise on the Law of Wreck and Salvage*, "Where the persons saved are slaves, and so property as well as persons, salvage is due."[54]

Capt. Sanderson of the *Surprize* later gave details of freeing the *Nimble*:

> Captain of the schooner requested me to haul alongside immediately to receive his [pivot] gun on board my vessel and get off the reef...finding that the rudder was entirely gone discovered there was no other method of getting her off the reef than but by lightening her; commenced throwing overboard the shot

[cannon balls] and kentledge [ballast], made a cable fast astern to my vessel, then made all sail and succeeded in checking the schooner round into deep water...the breeze freshening and the tide rising in about 30 minutes started the schooner from the bed of coral rock on which she lay...steered to the westward with the schooner in tow until I got her into three fathoms [18'] water.[55]

Lightship keeper Whalton early that morning sailed to the scene from his station in his ship's boat and met the *Surprize* towing the *Nimble*. He boarded the *Surprize* to assist the wreckers.

When Grover returned in his boat to the *Thorn* he found Gomez aboard! Gomez abandoned his half-submerged vessel to Grover, repeated he was not a prize to the British, and declared Grover "had the best right to her having first come to her assistance."[56] By his statement Gomez apparently was familiar with the ways and informal rules of the Florida Keys wreckers. He then begged Grover to protect him from the British, as if he, Gomez, was a victim, and to save the lives of the people aboard his wrecked ship.

Capt. Grover boarded on the *Thorn* 54 Spaniards and 246 Africans, females first. A fishing smack then arrived on the scene: the *Florida*, Capt. Austin Packer of Key West and Mystic River, Connecticut. Packer boarded 142 Africans and some 20 Spaniards on his schooner, which perhaps measured about 55' x 16' x 7' (the popular size of New England fishing vessels of the time).[57]

Guerrero's captain Joze Gomez saw before him that morning a warship stuck on the rocks some two miles away, $156,000 in human cargo (520 Africans worth $300 each in Havana), and three small vessels crewed by American simpletons. These were fishermen, and wreckers, that moored for weeks and months at low, uninhabited, rocky and swampy islets, swatting mosquitoes, waiting for someone to have an accident. Gomez commanded a slaver, was a pirate, and a bluffer, and then he became a hijacker.

While Grover waited for his "consort" Capt. Sanderson of the *Surprize* to arrive at the wreck from his exertions with the warship, the fishing smack *Florida* set sail, for Key West.

She arrived instead at Santa Cruz, Cuba, near Havana, the first vessel to be hijacked.

At 11:00, delayed because of a necessary repair to a sail damaged in pulling the warship off the rocks, the *Surprize* came to the slaver towing *Nimble*'s boat with Lt. Holland, mate Robert H. Elliot, and six seamen in it. All came onboard the *Thorn*. Holland's ship had been freed but she still could not sail without a rudder. Holland was a 26-year-old man of action, and was anticipating trouble by the slave traders, and did then what he could to ameliorate the situation. His intuition was astonishing, for he then had no knowledge of what was then happening at sea aboard the *Florida*. Nor would he for five more days.

He had all the loaded firearms onboard the *Thorn* that had been saved from the slaver discharged and others thrown overboard or otherwise disabled them with water ("dipped them into the sea").[58] At 12:00 the *Surprize* took aboard (by way of the boat from the *Nimble* and a boat from the slaver)[59] the remaining Spaniards, 12, and Africans, 122, who were all male.

Sanderson later related the ordeal of rescuing people from the wreck:

> The sea making...a clean breach over them,
> the slaves and crews being able to save
> themselves by holding on to ropes fastened
> for that purpose, they succeeded in saving all
> on board.[60]

How some 610 people survived the sea on a ship turned over on her side can perhaps be surmised by Sanderson's relation: they had been hanging from the rigging. It must have been an astounding sight.

The tension was very high. It became clear to all what the disposition of the Spaniards was. They could overpower the Americans. The *Thorn* did not sail for Key West - it was then 4:00 and night would be coming soon - but anchored next to the warship for the protection of her guns that evening, at the request of Lt. Holland. The *Surprize*, with only a handful of Spaniards aboard, remained two miles away near the wreck. Lightship Capt. John Whalton was terrified by the events, such as the disabling of the many guns, he had witnessed that day. After the *Thorn* left for the warship, he later reported,

> I then requested Capt. Sanderson to allow me to withdraw from his vessel as I expected she would be taken by the Spaniards. He acquiesced and I proceeded on board the lightboat.[61]

At a wind change at 6:00 the *Thorn*'s crew moved her slightly away from the warship to avoid fouling her cable with that of the *Nimble*'s. Lt. Holland hailed and asked what the crew was doing. At 8:00 Capt. Grover and most of the crew, after having given the watch "orders to keep a good lookout" went into the cabin for supper.

That was all the slave traders needed.

Chapter Five

December, 1827
Carysfort Reef and Santa Cruz

Second Hijacking to Cuba

The Spaniards cut the anchor line. The crew in the cabin heard their boat thumping against the hull and Nathaniel Glover and another sailor rushed out of the cabin, saw the vessel adrift, discovered the cut cable, and saw "the head of the jib [sail] running up" and dropped a second anchor over, "at which time I saw the main sail was hoisting up." Glover testified later:

> Several of the Spaniards jumped towards me. Then I ran off, when I found the companionway surrounded by the Spaniards. [I] jumped overboard [as did the other sailor],[62] swam to the man of war schooner, was picked up by the boat. I informed the officer in the boat that the *Thorn* was taken by the Spaniards. He went in pursuit of her a short distance, but finding it useless returned after firing several pistols.[63]

Capt. Grover and his pilot, Joseph Bethel, were confined to the cabin by the Spaniards, but Grover tried to go on deck anyway. He later related that he was met by

> The captain of the Spanish brig with a dirk and the doctor[64] of the brig with a pair of pistols and two men at the companion[way]

with cutlasses and pistols told him if he attempted to go on deck they would kill him.[65]

The *Thorn* sailed away. She too arrived at Santa Cruz. From the hijacked *Florida* and *Thorn* 398 Africans were marched into the Cuban countryside to join the 287,000 others enslaved in Cuba.[66]

Capt. Theophilus Conneau wrote the same year, 1827, of the procedure the slave traders of Cuba and the officials there used. From his memoirs (with my explanations in brackets):

I shall next narrate the manner they are landed in the Island of Cuba....

The landing of slaves is generally made now on some given point of the coast where the absence of habitation is apparent, but some hidden hut denotes the spot of the persons appointed to await the arrival. As soon as the anchor is let go, one or more boats are sent off and the landing is effected while some of the crew dismantle the vessel in order to avoid notice from inland or in the offing. Once the [human] cargo is landed, it is hastened in the interior as soon as possible, escorted by the Captain and part of the crew all well armed, and made to walk at a rapid rate. In this manner they are conducted to the nearest plantation whose consent is purchased before, and there deposited, which secures them from the grasping power of the petty magistrate of the district (called *capitan de partidos*) who in imitation of his superior the Governor would exact a remuneration for his consent [require bribe money].

In the meantime, a dispatch is sent to the owners in Havana, Matanzas, or Santiago de Cuba, who arrive post haste at the plantation with coarse dresses for the new-arrived Africans and the necessary gold to pay off the crew.

Messengers are sent off to the different slave brokers, who inform the needy purchaser that a quantity of Bossal [*bozal*, direct from Africa] slaves are to be disposed, mentioning the nation but not the owner, Captain, or the vessel that landed them. As gold is expected, nothing is said of the terms.

The vessel, if small, is either dismantled or so disfigured as to warrant a safe return in a port of clearance with a cargo of sugar or molasses and under the coasting flag.[67] But if the vessel is a brig or rigged ship, she is either burnt or sunk. Sometimes she is sent to St. Thomas, Curacao, or Spanish San Domingo as a distressed vessel, to appear again perhaps transmuted under another rig, paint, or name....[This may explain the changing of the name from *San Joze* to *Guerrero*.]

Should this be a cargo owned by a company, every one takes his share away with him to his house or plantation, but if owned by speculators who need them not, they are sold on the plantation to the planter who, gold in hand, chooses what best suits him. The operation of disposing of them is gone through with great a haste as possible, before the Great Britain Arugs [mythological giant with a hundred eyes] makes his report to the Governor General, who not in respect of

25

treaties but in fear of the Proud Albion Consul, promises to put the laws into force and with the dignity of a grandee of Spain orders the comandante of dragoons or lanceros to proceed at a gallop to the plantation designated by the representative of England, who awaits in person to see the order given.

While the sale takes place, one of the owners or his agent pays a morning visit to the Palacio, knows the Captain General's private secretary who is ever on attendance on such an occasion, and in comfortable vis-a-vis relates the happy landing of the contraband (such is the cognomen [nickname] given to the traffic), depositing in the meantime on the table the necessary rouleaux which contain the 51 dollars head money. As the man in the office draws the gold into the drawer with a patronizing manner, he offers a cigarillo to the cringing offerer who, hat in hands, awaits the order to depart. But not so, the gold is only for private purse of the Governor, the private factotum must have a share of the pie. But it must be done indirectly, and availing himself of the passing cloud of smoke he in an insinuating manner demands the price of a small slave which he has an immediate demand for. The hint is taken by the owner. In contraband transaction it is not only necessary to hold a candle to the Devil but to his imps also. Next morning a small slave is sent, or its equivalent in Spanish ounces, as it is well known that government officials prefer the gold to mortal flesh.[68]

Gomez allowed the *Florida* and *Thorn* to leave Santa

Cruz. He had a conversation onshore with Capt. Grover, and Grover said in a protest he made in Key West on December 26th[69] that Gomez "ordered him not to make sail until the following day." Was the *Thorn* being detained for perhaps another forced voyage, back to the Keys to get the other Africans? For the third vessel, the *Surprize*, had not appeared at Santa Cruz.

Grover's crew became especially terrified at what happened next; the threat of being killed. Crewmember William Wright later related that:

> The master of his schooner [Grover] went ashore with the Spaniards, and that during his absence reports reached the vessel that it was the intention of the said Spaniards to murder the crew during the night, being alarmed at which this deponent, with three American sailors named Thomas Smith, Acey Kingsbury, and John Gorman abandoned the schooner, and in the open boat sailed for this Port of Havana.

Once in Havana they told the story of the hijacking to the captain of the port, and then later to other officials, Wright believing one of them to be Captain-General Francisco Dionisio Vives.

The men were ordered back into their little boat and told to go out to sea but remain within gunshot of the port. The did so, but they defied the order, for the sea was rough. They came ashore in a small cove to the westward of Havana where they left the boat and came back into the city.

Back at Santa Cruz, with the assistance of Austin Packer, Grover, Bethel, and John Cargo got the *Thorn* underway, in company with the *Florida*.

After arriving at Key West Connecticut fisherman Austin Packer completely disappears from the ensuing depositions, protests, and other paperwork. Although Packer does appear in Key West history later as a wrecker, I feel that he wanted nothing further to do with anything connected to the slave ship. He had been fishing and came upon a horrible situation of desperate Africans and armed Cubans. Ten days later, on January 3, 1828, the schooner *Florida* left Savannah with Thomas Rooke of Indian Key as captain, bound for Key West.[70] Packer may have quickly sold his vessel to Rooke.

Chapter Six

December, 1827
Carysfort Reef

Armed: Fearing Another Hijacking

At Carysfort Reef another wrecker, the *General Geddes*, Capt. John Morrison, arrived at the scene a few hours before the hijacking of the *Thorn*. He saw the two ships while traveling up the reef at 2:00 p.m. on the 20th, "8 or 10 miles to the northward of the lightship." He was a regular consort of the other wreckers and was expected to be in the area - Capt. Grover had sent mate Nathaniel Glover in a boat to look for him at 1:00 p.m. that day.

At 4:00 Capt. Morrison anchored 1/4 mile from the *Nimble*, then spoke to Capt. Grover on his way to the warship (for the protection offered), who told him to go to the slaver and save what he could. Aboard Grover's vessel were Lt. Holland and a few of his men, and it is possibly from them that Morrison sensed that he was coming into a dangerous situation. Morrison later testified that he

> Immediately dispatched the boat for sloop *Capital*, also a consort, to come to my assistance, got underway and anchored close to the sloop *Surprize*, Capt. Sanderson. Finding that he had a great many negroes and Spaniards on board and knowing their disposition well I determined to lay alongside of him during the night to protect him as he is also a consort. Ordered my crew to get the arms ready to protect the *Surprize* and my own vessel which was done.

About 9:00 discovered a boat under my stern and expecting the Spaniards had risen ordered him to keep off and inform me who she was or I would fire into her....I was then informed that the schooner *Thorn* was taken by the Spaniards and I expected they had taken possession of the sloop *Surprize*. I then requested the [British] officer to take a few of my men and go alongside and see if all was well onboard [the *Surprize*]. When he returned he reported all on board was well with the exception of two men being wounded.

There is no explanation in the documents as to what led to the wounding of the *Surprize*'s men. Samuel Sanderson testified that

Night coming on, two of my people having been wounded; one by a pistol ball and the other by a stabber knife I was unable to get my vessel underway. The schooner *General Geddes*, Capt. John Morrison also being a consort of mine came to anchor close by me which encouraged me to lay there until morning as I knew he had a strong crew and could protect me. At daylight in the morning of the 21st weighed anchor and made sail for Key West, at the same time discovering the disposition on the part of the Spaniards to mutiny and take my vessel from me, I ran down to the schooner *Nimble* and anchored close alongside her and requested the commander of said vessel to take them out. Ten was taken out...He put on board of me one officer and four men with arms.[71]

Even though there were only 22 Spaniards left that morning (12 on the *Surprize* and 10 that had been taken as prisoners to the warship at an unknown time) Lt. Holland was apprehensive too of another hijacking. Nathaniel Glover had stayed the night on the warship after being hauled out of the water by her crew and later related:

> The next morning about 8:00 the sloop *Surprize* came down, was hailed by the captain of the man of war, and cried where she was bound. The reply was, to Key West. He ordered her to come to anchor immediately or he would fire into her. They answered that they would anchor as soon as she cleared the shoals. He then ordered his men to go and discharge three muskets at her. The shot went through the mainsail, carried away the top at the head of the jib. The sloop then anchored and was boarded by the man of war, who took to her all of the crew of the Spanish Guineaman but two.[72]

Holland apparently thought the *Surprize* was being hijacked; hence the gunfire. The Africans were under his charge, his protection. Losing more of them to slavery in Cuba would be a horrendous failure of duty.

The *Surprize* then sailed for Key West. (Later Holland wrote that he had "engaged" - hired - the wreckers to take the Africans to Key West. None of the wreckers' testimonies confirm that.)[73]

Apparently two *Guerrero* crewmen were actually brought into Key West by the *Surprize*. One wonders whatever became of them, and why they were allowed to stay with the Americans. It is possible they were American crewmen on the Spanish ship. Or, that they were responsible for the woundings and the Americans wanted them held to punishment by American law. I have found nothing further on their fate.

John Walker, master of another aptly-named wrecker, the *Capital*, arrived after being summoned by Morrison's men who came to Tavernier Key, a wrecker's station, to find him. He arrived at Carysfort Reef about 8:00 a.m. After the *Surprize* sailed there were only the rudderless *Nimble*, the *General Geddes*, and the *Capital* at the site of the wreck, and wrecking became the order of the day. Morrison directed Walker to work the slaver while two of his crew who were carpenters fitted the *Nimble* with the rudder from the *Guerrero*, which took 30 hours to do. Walker saved some of the sails and *Guerrero*'s fourteen cannon, four of them brass,[74] her boats, anchors, rigging, and dry goods.[75] The British were also salvaging the wreck in their boat during Morrison's exertions with the *Nimble*'s rudder.

The temporary repair finally completed - Morrison declared in a deposition the rudder "fitted well" - the *Nimble* and the *General Geddes* sailed for Key West at 8:00 a.m. on the 23rd, arriving at dark on Christmas Eve.[76] On Christmas Day the *Florida* and the *Thorn* arrived there.[77] The *Surprize* had arrived at Key West on December 22nd.

Chapter Seven

December, 1827 - March, 1828
Key West, Florida

Fear & Legal Arguments
at an Island Village

One of the Africans died on the *Surprize* before or during the voyage down the island chain to Key West.[78] Key West was then a small village of 421 people[79] and the only non-Indian settlement at all in the peninsula south of St. Augustine and the plantation area of Northeast Florida. The dominant structure seen on the island by the Africans would have been the 67' lighthouse built the year before.[80] Many - some 100 - of the residents were fishermen from the Mystic River, Connecticut, area who were at Key West only in the winter, living on their vessels.[81] Two years before it was stated by a visitor that there was only one comfortable house on the island,[82] the other houses apparently were rather primitive.

The Collector of Customs, William Pinkney, wrote the Secretary of the Treasury, Richard Rush, in charge of Customs, the day after the Africans arrived:

> The balance of the slaves 121 in number were put on board the sloop *Surprize* of this port who has brought them here & delivered a manifest of them. I have thought it my duty to seize them and now hold them subject to the disposition of the President. I have placed them in charge of the deputy marshal here, and it is proper that clothing should be provided for

33

them as they are nearly naked & liable to perish with cold. I have directed the deputy marshal to purchase provisions & sufficient blankets to protect them from the cold.[83]

When Lt. Holland arrived he and the Key Westers sparred. First of all, the Collector of Customs, Pinkney, wanted the custody of the Africans on the grounds that they had landed in US territory from a ship wrecked on the reef. But Holland saw them as under the protection of the British government for the slave ship they had been on had surrendered to him (the showing of the light).

Pinkney also wanted the British to pay duties on the items and equipment saved by them from the slaver they were importing into US territory. He may even have told Lt. Holland the law's penalty for non-compliance: the loss of his ship.[84]

Lt. Holland did not intend to land any of the items saved on American shores so disagreed with Pinkney's view on the duties as well as on the protection of the Africans.

But most of all it was the wreckers' intentions on receiving a large salvage award that brought strife, for Lt. Holland apparently knew the reputation of the townspeople and resisted them.

Today it is called "Bubbaism" in Key West but collusion was common in the Key West of the 1820s as well. Residents helped themselves and each other to profiteer.

The men of Key West had a law, passed by the government of the Territory of Florida just four years before, that seemed fair on paper but which certainly was not in practice. Salvage awards would be determined by a "Court of Arbitrators" consisting of five men, two of whom the hapless ship captain was to appoint but who were generally appointed for him. Two would be appointed by the salvors and the other by the notary public. One can assume there was much winking and elbow nudging as the "court" members awarded their fellow citizens 50-90 percent of the value of the salvaged ship and cargo. Holland would not submit the question of salvage to the "arbitrators" set-up, later writing, "I could hardly expect to be fairly treated when the arbitrators...were, nearly, part owners engaged in the wrecking vessels."[85]

Ships had actually been sold at Key West just to pay the salvage awards...and Lt. Holland was not, *NOT*, going to lose a British warship to the Key Westers!!!!

After three days of Holland's arguing with the locals *Nimble*'s men hoisted anchor on December 27th and the British sailed away, without paying the wreckers a single dime.

Some of the final communications between the British and Americans follows:

[Lt. Holland onboard the *Nimble* to William Pinkney]

Key West
26th December, 1827

Sir,

Upon receipt of your letter of yesterday's date, I have withdrawn the officers and men from the negroes now at Key West and whom I consider unjustly detained.

With regard to that part of your letter concerning the payment or securing the duties on wrecked goods, I can only repeat that as I look upon them as British property and onboard a vessel of war I do not conceive myself called upon to pay any duties upon them, [but] am willing to give the security you may deem expedient for the payment thereof should it be decided that I have taken a wrong view of this subject.[86]

[Lt. Holland to the Principal Magistrate at Key West - George E. Tingle was the Justice of the Peace and would have been the recipient of this letter.]

December 26, 1827

Sir,

The master of the American sloop *Surprize* having refused to deliver the gun belonging to this schooner to one of my officers which he holds in his possession I have to request you will be pleased to inform me if this procedure is agreeable to the American law; if not, what steps may be taken immediately to have the gun restored.

[The Key West firm of Bunce and Disney to Lt. Holland, apparently acting as agent for the wreckers and, perhaps unknown to Lt. Holland, owners of the *Thorn*.[87]]

26th December, 1827

We received your note of this morning and have conversed with the gentlemen on the subject of salvage. They inform us they are willing to accept your proposition so far as related to the schooner under your command but they cannot concede the [slaver] brig ought to be placed in a similar situation. They are willing the [arbitrators] court should decide if it was a prize to you or not.

[Lt. Holland to Bunce & Disney]

26th December, 1827
Key West

Gentlemen:

As I feel it my duty not to allow the salvage to be settled by arbitration when a competent tribunal can be refered to, I can only offer my former proposition and request the gentlemen concerned will come to a final decision it being my wish to sail tomorrow.[88]

The proposition was simply this, written by Holland:

I am willing to sign any bond or security for the sum awarded by any competent tribunal in the United States for salvage of the above mentioned schooner and brig shall be duly paid and the statement of both parties shall be forwarded to enable a court to decide.[89]

[John Morrison to Lt. Holland]

27th December

Sir,

The salvage in the case of HBM schooner *Nimble* not having yet been adjusted and understanding it is your intention to proceed to sea without a final settlement of same I thought proper, in hopes it may alter your determination, to recapitulate to you the hardships of the case.

You are well aware, sir, that your situation on the reef was very perilous and but for my timely assistance there is great doubt whether your vessel would have been saved. You are also well aware but for my exertions you would not have been able to procure a rudder which in all probability would have detained you a considerable time in port and would have put you to great expense in fitting your vessel for sea.

Your boats were employed in wrecking the brig which could easily have been done by me while I was putting your vessel in a situation to proceed to sea. I was told the British government would pay me more than I could save; and relying upon your honor as an officer I continued my exertions....

My vessel cost me $8,000 which was at stake in this business and I was compelled in consequence of being onboard of your vessel to employ a stranger to bring her down. All of these circumstances I think I am entitled to a little rate of salvage and hope you would take some steps before you leave here to settle it in amicable terms.

[Lt. Holland to John Morrison]

Key West
December 27th, 1827

Sir,

Having made known to you my determination more than 24 hours ago concerning the mode in which the salvage should be settled both for HBM Schooner *Nimble* and [slaver] brig, I do not feel myself called upon to wait any longer at this port as yesterday you were well aware of my intention to sail this day. I shall forward a statement of the facts to the British Vice-Admiral, and now pledge to you my word that any decision any competent court should come to I will abide by it. I cannot positively promise you, but I think it more than probable that either myself or some other British vessel of war will shortly be sent to fulfill my obligation.

With regard to making the rudder you are aware my boat was sent for it and doubtless would have got it without your assistance. I acknowledge your attentive and valuable assistance in bringing me to this port which shall be properly mentioned in my statement to the British Vice-Admiral but I have no doubt I could have saved the schooner without being towed off by the *Surprize* as that happened before high water [high tide] and I had an anchor to windward to prevent driving further on the reef. I comprehend everything of any value was saved from the wreck, before we sailed....and now, the last moment wholly elapsed which I can possibly spare must conclude.[90]

Lt. Holland wrote a month later to Vice-Admiral Charles E. Fleming:

January 28, 1828

Port Royal [Jamaica]

I thought it better not to waste time in making bargains with them and consequently determined to having the affair settled by the decisions of the admiralty court; I made this my determination known to the salvors immediately upon my arrival at Key West[91] and requested their speedy decision as I was anxious to sail. They at first positively refused and after waiting two days I told them I should sail the following evening at 4:00 whether they agreed or not. I had offered to sign any paper...to secure to them the payment of any sum which should be awarded by any competent tribunal for their assistance...

At 4:00 when I was weighing my anchor the parties concerned came on board and requested me to enter into a bond for $15,000 that they should be paid by the British government...This I refused to sign.

I did not think it proper to wait, after what I had told them the day before, and therefore sailed immediately; it may not be amiss to say that I engaged a pilot to take me out over the reef and on leaving the schooner the wreckers persuaded him to leave us, evidently hoping thereby either to detain me or that I might get ashore it being a foul wind. I beat out in the night without any accident, however. [92]

The *Nimble* did get her cannon back from the *Surprize*. And then the British were gone; leaving the Africans at Key West. Should Holland and the Key Westers not have had the arguments he would have taken the Africans to Havana, where the Mixed Commission Court surely would have declared them free. But their treatment in Cuba as declared *emancipados* ("freed people") would have been as other Africans rescued from slave ships in Cuba was: they would have been worked as if they *were* enslaved.[93]

What happened next at Key West was related in an anonymous letter written on the island:

> The schooner *Thorn* and the smack *Florida*, which had been risen upon by the crew of the Spanish brig, returned [to Key West] on the 25th, having landed the Negroes which they had on board at Santa Cruz. A report reached us, a few days since that a Spanish armed brig was fitting [out] in Havana, to come to this place for the purpose of taking away the Negroes which had been saved from the wreck, and brought in here. We soon put the island in a state of defence - on the North side of it we mounted 4 brass 12's, a little to the Eastward we had 8 iron 6's and in the middle of the leading street [then Whitehead St.] we planted two 12 lb. Carronades - our militia was ordered out and kept under arms nearly all night - had they come they would have met with a warm reception. But nearly a week elapsed; there was probably no truth in the report.[94]

The concern was certainly warranted, however. The

Africans in Key West, if sold at Havana, would bring over $36,000. The "4 brass 12's" were certainly the 4 brass 12-pounder cannons that John Walker of the *Capital* had taken off the wreck of the *Guerrero*. The Key Westers were preparing to shoot the Cuban slave traders with their very own cannon.

Besides that to worry about the wreckers thought - in error - that Pinkney should be worried about too. On January 5th they wrote to Secretary of State Henry Clay the circumstances of the rescue of the Africans and non-payment by the British and, they

> Have been informed and believe that the collector of this port, William Pinkney, Esquire, either has or intends to set up a claim against the United States for the bounty allowed to citizens for capturing vessels laden with negroes from the coast of Africa or thereby assuming to himself the attitude of your memorialists and excluding them from all benefit, or emoluments if any there be realized from the capture, if it may be so called.[95]

Three months later a letter written by the US marshal in St. Augustine, Waters Smith, to Secretary Rush, requesting reimbursement of his own funds expended on behalf of the Africans relates more terror at Key West:

> I had the honor of addressing you, on the 8th of February last, on the subject of 121 African Negroes, then in my custody at Key West. I have since removed them to this place [St. Augustine] for greater safety. While they were at Key West, attempts were made to take them from the possession of my deputy, by force, and by bribery; and, the night before I removed them from the island, an attempt was

made to carry off a part of them. Capt. [Josiah] Doane, of the [US] revenue cutter *Marion* assisted me, with one of his officers and part of his crew, to protect the Africans; and, on a requisition from Colonel Pinkney and myself, convoyed the vessel in which I transported the Negroes, from Key West, to this place. I deemed it absolutely necessary to remove the Negroes from Key West: they were not safe there; but the removal was attended with considerable expense: they were placed in my custody perfectly naked, many of them sick and extremely weak and feeble: it was necessary to clothe them, and humanity required that medical aid should be furnished the sick. I have...for their removal, clothing, medical attendance, and rations, paid upwards of three thousand dollars.[96]

Waters Smith had been alerted to the situation by his deputy in Key West, Fielding A. Browne.[97] William Pinkney had turned the custody of the Africans over to the deputy. (By law Africans rescued from slave ships were to be in the custody of a US Marshal.) Browne's letter did not reach the marshal in St. Augustine until January 28th. Waters Smith was familiar with Key West. He had sailed down there before over some "strange doings" on the island.[98]

In another letter Marshal Waters Smith relates that attentive medical care was given to the Africans in Key West:

About thirty of the number [were] sick with dysentery and a disease of the eyes, which Col. Pinkney the Collector observes "without [so] much care and attention would have probably resulted in the total loss of sight among numbers of them" and with all the attention which could be bestowed, three of the number are entirely blind, and two partially so. My deputy immediately wrote to me that he was under constant apprehension of losing the negroes, as it would be an easy matter for the owners in Cuba, to take them off.[99]

How and where 121 Africans lived in Key West is unknown, for Key West had no newspaper at the time (and because of that no other historian has discovered this dramatic time in Key West's history). In the 75 days the Africans were at Key West they might have been quartered in merchandise storehouses owned by Pardon C. Greene, a man rumored to be a retired slave trader (and who Greene Street in Key West is named for) which had been built by 1825 or they may have lived in barracks fronting the harbor between Duval and Whitehead streets which were built about 1824.[100]

In 2004 I handled a vessel's manifest in a North Florida archive that astounded me. It was dated at Alexandria, Virginia, February 15, 1828:

> Report and manifest of the cargo of slaves on board the sloop *Telegraph* of Key West - whereof William Loosemore is master, burthen 23 & 28/95 tons - bound from the Port of Alexandria in the District of Columbia for St. Marks...

Loosemore, previously unknown in Key West history, was transporting 16 enslaved African-Americans (for one Samuel Culver and one Aaron Dyer) to St. Marks in the Florida panhandle.[101] Resolutions had been presented to Congress in December, 1827 and January, 1828 and were acted on by January 21, to improve the channel at St. Marks, declare it a port of entry, and build a lighthouse. It is probable that the enslaved aboard Loosemore's sloop were intended to work on the channel, and it is also probable that he stopped at his vessel's home port of Key West in the voyage from Virginia to St. Marks and was the man Waters Smith wrote about that "by force, and bribery" tried to abduct the Africans (and put them on his sloop bound to St. Marks).

Thanks to Browne, Smith, Pinkney, and Capt. Doane the Africans finally were away from Key West and nearby Havana. They left March 7th and arrived at St. Augustine March 11th. But they were still not out of harm's way.

Only 114 arrived at St. Augustine;[102] six had died at Key West. One African was taken and kept by Capt. Doane onboard the revenue cutter, perhaps for a servant. Those who died would have been buried in the sand at Key West's potter's field, now named Higgs Beach, where hundreds more Africans rescued from the *Wildfire* and two other slave ships also enroute to Cuba were buried in 1860.[103] It is a place, now a county park, that has a tragic history.

Chapter Eight

January, 1828
Havana

Evading Spain's Law:
398 Lost to Slavery

On January 12, 1828 the *Surprize* arrived in Havana.[104] Samuel Sanderson's reason for going there is not known, but perhaps it was to complain to Cuban authorities about the hijackings of his consorts, or to sell equipment and goods salvaged from the *Guerrero*. He would have to be most careful in doing so as Gomez was ruthless, but it could have been accomplished through brokers very familiar with the wrecking business and friendly to the Americans of Key West. Another reason he was there could have been to try again to be paid salvage by Lt. Holland. Sanderson had pulled the *Nimble* off the reef *and* rescued Africans, so was doubly due salvage, he may have thought.

Holland sailed to Havana to deliver the Spanish prisoners onboard his warship[105] to authorities for justice through the Mixed Commission Court. When the *Nimble* arrived there *Thorn* crewmember William Wright, who was from Londonderry, Ireland, and a British subject, applied to Lt. Holland, who took him on as a crewmember. The other three *Thorn* sailors, all Americans, went aboard an American warship also in port in Havana, the *Natchez*.[106]

When Holland arrived he informed Captain-General Vives of the circumstances and the landing of recaptured Africans (a term used for those saved from slave ships) on the island's shore. Holland also informed British Commissioners Kilbee and Macleay. They immediately

46

questioned under oath William Wright. They wrote to London on January 3rd:

> Being in possession of such unquestionable evidence to the fact of the clandestine disembarkation of Negroes on this Island, we judged it to be our duty to address a representation to the Captain General apprizing him of all the circumstances of the case, and enclosing him a copy of Wright's deposition, and we informed him at the same time where the latter, and the three American sailors, who had come with him, were to be found. We concluded to expressing our confident hope that the information which we had given His Excellency [Vives] would enable him to trace out the Negroes in order that the benefit of emancipation, to which they had an undoubted right, might be conferred upon them.

> We have the honor to enclose a copy of our Note to the Captain General, together with a translation of his reply. In the latter your Lordship will find fully exemplified what we have elsewhere stated respecting the conduct of His Excellency in similar cases. Instead, as might naturally be expected, of his availing himself of the information which we transmitted, for the purpose of discovering, by enquires from the authorities and others upon the spot, whether such disembarkation had taken place, and if so, of ascertaining where the Negroes had been removed; he informs us that he has sent our note, together with a letter which he had himself received from Lieut. Holland, to one of his legal assessors for his opinion thereupon.[107]

Spain's laws were again avoided by the governor of Cuba; the fate of the 398 illegally landed Africans was sealed the moment they arrived on his island. Historian Hugh Thomas refers to it all as a "labyrinth of evasion."[108] Vives did assure the Commissioners, however, that he had ordered that the 20 *Guerrero* crewmembers that Holland had delivered for justice "to be placed in prison, where they are in perfect security to await the results of the proceedings."[109]

But the Court had no jurisdiction over owners or crewmembers of slave ships, only over the ship itself. It is likely they were later released.

HBM *Nimble* was not at Havana when the *Surprize* arrived. The warship had come into port in "a disabled state"[110] and sailed for Port Royal, Jamaica for repairs on January 2nd, arriving there on January 15th.[111]

Chapter Nine

January, 1828
Charleston, South Carolina

The Wreckers' Plea for Payment

The standard verbalism used by the Florida Keys wreckers upon speaking with the captain of a ship aground was, "Do you request assistance?" And now, the wreckers themselves requested assistance - assistance in getting paid for their efforts, for the terror they went through with the armed Cubans and the hijackings, for saving hundreds of Africans from the sea, and particularly, for getting a British warship freed from the reef *and* sailing again.

Whatever their financial intentions were in those efforts it cannot be emphasized too highly that without their work all the people aboard the *Guerrero* - African and Spanish - some 610 people - would have probably perished on the wreck. The coast was uninhabited and six miles away in a sea churned by stormy weather. Water was not easily found on the Keys - one had to know where the rare fresh water springs were to survive. If the Spaniards in their boats had made it to the warship they would have been taken prisoner, so that was not a likely scenario, and transporting the hundreds of Africans to the *Nimble* - a disabled ship over two miles away - would have been difficult, if the vessel could have even held 610 people - and the *Nimble*'s water supply was very low at the time.[112] The lightship was miles away; land was closer, and, even if the lightship was reached, it had limited supplies for the number of men, usually six or less, aboard her. What would have happened without the intervention of the wreckers and the fishing

49

smack is almost unimaginable.

Wrecker John Morrison was probably particularly angry over non-payment of salvage as Holland had told him at the wreck site that "I need not save anything from the brig as the British government would pay me threefold."[113] Morrison was from Charleston. His vessel was named for a former governor of South Carolina, General John Geddes, who was also a Charleston resident.

Geddes had once owned Key West. He had sent his brother George Washington Geddes and brother in law Dr. Benjamin R. Montgomery down to the island in March, 1822 to physically claim it. He had purchased it in 1821 from John B. Strong of St. Augustine, who had purchased it from the island's Spanish owner, Juan Pablo Salas, also of St. Augustine. John Simonton, also having purchased the island from Salas, had arrived in Key West and claimed it two months before, in January, 1822. John Geddes went in person to Key West with family members in August, 1822. Apparently ignoring the legal issue of ownership or because of it Dr. Montgomery had a house built on Key West (later purchased by Pardon C. Greene and probably the one "comfortable" house on the island) but, contracting yellow fever, died at Key West the next year, which resulted in a further, tragic, connection to the island of Key West for Geddes. Montgomery's tombstone in a Charleston churchyard is inscribed, "Died at Key West."[114]

Geddes' business partner in Charleston was Charles Edmonston, a wharf owner who was also very familiar with the Keys. Early in 1827 he had purchased a part of Key Vaca, in the Middle Florida Keys. The two mens' relationship with John Morrison is unknown, but Geddes was a director of a Charleston bank, which may have financed Morrison's *General Geddes*.

On January 15, 1828, the schooner *Lilly* arrived at Charleston from Key West after a four day sail. Cargo onboard was wrecked goods of cotton and crockery assigned to Asa C. Tift (another Key Wester) and C. Edmonston, indicating that Edmonston was not just a Key Vaca property owner but also was involved in the Key West wrecking business.

Lilly's Capt. John Sawyer brought news that at Key West when he left were the *General Geddes*, *Capital*, and *Surprize*, bound to "Cape Florida in a few days." (The term "Cape Florida" at the time meant the uppermost Keys area. The term was used for the entire end of the Florida peninsula until the late 1700s, when two surveyors made the place name an issue between them.)

Sawyer made no mention of where Austin Packer's *Florida* was (of interest since Sawyer was from Mystic River as well) nor of the location of the *Thorn*. The three wreckers mentioned were obviously headed back to the wreck of the *Guerrero* to do more salvaging. They then must have sailed directly to Charleston, for by January 25th John Geddes and Charles Edmonston had a letter written to Secretary of State Henry Clay, as "agents" of the wreckers Morrison, Walker, Sanderson, and Grover.

It was an eloquent letter. Enclosed were individual depositions by the wreckers taken by Justice of the Peace George E. Tingle in Key West on January 7th. Also in the letter's package were depositions of Carysfort lightship keeper John Whalton and three Key West residents who became involved. This letter and enclosures was forwarded to the British minister in Washington by Secretary Clay in 1828, and reposed in an archive in London where my researcher Andrea Cordani read it into a tape for me in 1992.

The following is excerpted from Geddes' and Edmonston's letter:

> From an attentive perusal of the documents we are under the deepest conviction that highly meritorious services have been rendered by the memorialists both to His Britannic Majesty's Schooner *Nimble*...and to the Spanish brig *Guerrero* and the people that were saved from the wreck of the latter, and that the

51

memorialists are richly entitled to liberal compensation for those services... rendered to [England's] man of war at much risk, labor and loss of time...[if] situations such as that in which the *Nimble* was placed when relieved by the memorialists are not to be properly compensated, [then] the adventurous and hardy class of men that devote themselves for livelihood to such undertakings could ill afford to bestow such services and perhaps no nation [more than England, with her vast sea traffic through the Straits of Florida from Jamaica] would feel the result more sensibly if for want of proper encouragement [if] these pursuits were abandoned....

They venture to think that the British government are bound by the pledge of their officer...[115]

By the time Henry Clay received this letter from Charleston he had become familiar with the *Nimble* and *Guerrero* by way of another complaint - that of the British Minister in Washington, Charles Vaughan, who had received a letter from Lt. Holland, written while Holland was in Havana. Vaughan asked Clay that Holland be relieved of any further proceedings on behalf of the Key West Collector of Customs and that the Africans be surrendered.

Vaughan was very familiar with the slave trade to Cuba, for he had formerly been the British minister to Spain, and had been active in that position in promoting the anti-slave trade treaty between the Spanish and British.[116]

President John Quincy Adams first became involved in the British/American affair when Secretary of the Treasury Richard Rush brought him two letters from William Pinkney written in December on trying to collect duties and the custody of the Africans. Adams responded that the British should have paid the duties, but since they had sailed there was nothing to do. As for the Africans, Rush wrote Pinkney on February 7th:

> The President directs that you keep them in custody and provide for their necessary wants, in as economical a manner as circumstances may allow, until you receive final instructions as to the way in which they are to be disposed of from the Navy Department...It will be proper that you take a list of the slaves, noting the age of each as far as you may be enabled to do so.[117]

The list apparently did not survive a Treasury Department fire in 1833.

It had been the next day that Waters Smith wrote to Rush from St. Augustine, on the danger to the Africans at Key West.

> The length of time that is required to receive an answer to a letter from Washington has determined me to proceed at once to Key West and bring the negroes to this place where they will be perfectly secure until some disposition shall be made of them. For that purpose I have chartered a vessel and sailed this day for Key West.[118]

Washington was then receiving complaints and reports from all over - Charleston, Havana, St. Augustine - on the events of late December at Key West.

Adams and Secretary Clay had a conversation on the situation. Clay responded to Minister Vaughan on February 18th. The duties law passed by Congress on March 3, 1825 had been violated by Lt. Holland, he wrote:

> In carrying away the goods in contrary to the explicit provision of this act, and after being

admonished of its existence by the collector
of Key West, Lt. Holland has subjected
himself to censure...[119]

As to the custody of the Africans, Lt. Holland should
not have tried to capture the slave ship in US territorial
waters. Clay was apologetic; "Such is the view which the
undersigned regrets the President has been compelled to
take," he wrote. Custody of the Africans by the Americans
was proper because of that violation. Adams thought
perhaps the courts would be involved should Great Britain
challenge American custody, and, if so, "the negroes will be
detained a reasonable time" to allow an opportunity for a
court test. In either case, whether under American or British
custody,

The condition of the unfortunate Africans
will be the same, if the laws of Great Britain
are correctly understood; that is, they will be
restored as free men to their native country.
By retaining them, the United States assumes
the expense of their support and
transportation to their country.[120]

The laws of Great Britain - that nation's anti-slave
trade treaties with Spain - were *not* correctly understood.
Although Africans aboard slave ships captured off the
African coast were taken to Sierra Leone on the African
continent those captured on ships off Cuba, at least during
this time period, were taken to Cuba to be emancipated.
Such was the terminology, at least, the Africans' liberty
being far from real.
  Clay had been an organizing member of the private
American Colonization Society (official name, "American
Society for Colonizing the Free People of Color of the
United States"), which supported a settlement on the West
Coast of Africa which came to be named Liberia - land of
the liberated - established for free and freed American blacks

six years before, in 1822.

On the same date, February 18, 1828, but under a separate cover Clay wrote to Vaughan on the salvage claim of the wreckers. Vaughan replied he had not heard from Lt. Holland on any settlement, and would forward Clay's papers (received from Charleston) to the admiral commanding His Majesty's naval force in the West Indies.

Vaughan's reply to Clay on the matter of the payment of duties and the "illegal capture" cited by President Adams through Clay was contained disbelief:

> It appears to the undersigned that the act [requiring payment of duties] does not apply to prize goods on board one of His Majesty's vessels of war.

And, on the capture,

> The undersigned cannot agree...Great Britain and...the United States are engaged in the exercise of maritime police for the suppression of the crime of trading in slaves, and their operations in the future cannot but be embarrassed by the declaration that the pursuit of their common enemy, the dealer in slaves, must cease whenever he must place himself within the territorial jurisdiction of one of the powers not actually engaged in the pursuit....

And, on the Africans,

> With regard to the offer of the Secretary of State to detain the Negroes for a reasonable time, should it be thought advisable to obtain a decision of a court of justice, the undersigned does not think it expedient to accept that offer.

By the end of February 1828 the Africans, then still in Key West, were officially given up by the British, Pinkney's demand of duties from Lt. Holland declared correct by the President and incorrect by the British Minister, and the wreckers' complaint of non-payment was being forwarded from Minister Vaughan in Washington to British Royal Navy Vice-Admiral of the White, Charles E. Fleming.

Chapter Ten

1828 – 1829
Northeast Florida

Plantation Slavery   ·

There is an ancient stone fort at the harbor of St. Augustine, completed in 1695. St. Augustine is the nation's oldest continually occupied city, dating to 1565, decades before Jamestown and Plymouth were settled. It had been a Spanish city, established to protect the treasure fleets that sailed back to Spain past Florida. The coquina shellstone fort was begun in 1672, because of a pirate raid on the town in 1668. It was designed something like a medieval fortress, complete with a moat.[121]

I wondered, upon seeing it from their perspective, if the Africans were fearful that they were being brought to a slave fortress, those hellish dungeons built by Europeans on the African coast used in the "trade."

In 1828 it was a tiny American city. Ornithologist John James Audubon, passing through in 1831, described St. Augustine as "the poorest hole in the Creation...the country around nothing but bare sand hills - hot one day cold another."[122] He was right about the temperature extremes, and didn't note the heavy rainfall endured by those living there.

Despite the fact that bringing the Africans into St. Augustine was none other than the former mayor of St. Augustine, and then US Marshal of the Eastern District of Florida, Waters Smith, on John Morrison's sleek vessel the *General Geddes*, and escorted by a US revenue cutter, the *Marion*, Deputy Collector of Customs Thomas F. Cornell was suspicious (and, probably, elated). He believed these Africans were being imported into the United States illegally, and did not allow the *General Geddes* to anchor in port, although he did allow the Africans to disembark, "A representation having been made to me that these negroes were in an unhealthy state, arising from their confinement on board the vessel" he wrote to Secretary Rush March 15th. He wrote Rush that Capt. Morrison had an affidavit that

> The slaves brought to this port in his vessel had been taken from the wreck of a Spanish slave brig, found on the Florida reef. Waters Smith, Esq. Marshal for this District, also made an affidavit before me, that the negroes were brought to this place for safe keeping....No evidence is adduced before me, other than the oath of the Captain, that these slaves were taken from a wreck...

Which was not quite true - Morrison had presented a manifest of the Africans signed off by the Collector in Key West, Pinkney. What Deputy Collector of Customs Cornell was really writing to Rush about was money. He continued:

> I addressed a letter (not officially) to the District Attorney of the United States, informing him that these negroes had been brought into the Territory, and requested him to adopt the legal measures pointed out in the act of Congress of 3d March, 1819, entitled "An act in addition to the acts prohibiting the slave trade," under which I claim the bounty therein authorized to an informer.[123]

The District Attorney he wrote to was Thomas Douglas, another St. Augustine resident who was quite fond of Waters Smith. It is doubtful Douglas gave Cornell's letter serious thought. Cornell was hoping for the bounty allowed to informers by the 1819 statute for each illegally imported African rescued from slavery and delivered to a US marshal. (This is the bounty the wreckers believed Pinkney would request.) The problem here in St. Augustine was, of course, that the Africans were already in custody of a US marshal!

While at Key West Marshal Smith was approached by one of the Africans, named Lewis, who had his son with him, age about 12. In July Smith wrote the Secretary of the Navy Samuel L. Southard from St. Augustine:

> This man is the son of an African residing on that part of the coast resorted to by slave vessels; he speaks French and Spanish very well, and can make himself understood in English; he has been over to Havana in a slave vessel as Interpreter, and was hired in the same situation by the master of the Brig *Guerrero* at thirty dollars per month. This information is obtained from Lewis, and also from the captain of the slave brig [apparently before the hijackings]: he took his son with him on board the Brig; they were not a part of the slave cargo. Lewis is desirous of going to Havana to receive the wages due him; from whence he states that he can get a passage to Africa. He applied to me at Key West for permission to go to Havana.
>
> Lewis is a smart, intelligent negro, but void of principal, is dissatisfied at being retained here, and having great influence over the other Negroes, is constantly exciting [them] in a way that gives me much trouble: I have once been compelled to confine him in irons.
>
> It would relieve me from considerable anxiety if I could be authorized to allow him to go to Havana either with or without his son, but I

do not feel myself justified in doing so without permission from the Government.

Will you be pleased Sir, to favor me with instructions on this subject.[124]

Other Africans had been liberated from slave ships in US waters, and delivered to US marshals who eventually were reimbursed for their expenses. Smith believed he would be as well. But to check his financial outlay he hired out the Africans - as slaves - to area plantations. He later was ordered from Washington to do just that.

Those too young to work Smith placed with St. Augustine families. There were 89 Africans in the group that could work. Of that number it is known that 36 were hired out to Zephaniah Kingsley and 20 to Joseph M. Hernandez.

The Kingsley Plantation, on Fort George Island 22 miles east of Jacksonville and just north of the St. Johns River, was one of several properties Kingsley owned. He moved there in 1814. It still exists, and is now a National Park Service site. The ruins of slave houses built perhaps in the 1820s (date of constructions is uncertain) can be seen there today. Kingsley had been a slave trader. One of his importations of enslaved Africans was as the owner of the vessel *Superior*, bringing 250 to Havana in 1802.[125] Other voyages, to Florida, by Kingsley with lesser numbers of enslaved people are known.[126] By the time the *Guerrero* people arrived Kingsley owned some 200 enslaved people. And it was opportune for him that the *Guerrero* people should arrive just at a time when he needed even more laborers.

Kingsley had signed a contract in January, 1828 with the US government to deepen a nearby channel through some oyster beds which would improve the shipping of the products of his plantation as well as navigation for others.[127] It was certainly labor intensive and terrible work, and this is likely the work the Africans were assigned.

Joseph M. Hernandez also badly needed laborers at the time as well. While the Africans were still in Key West this news item was printed in the January 18, 1828 *Pensacola Gazette*:

St. Augustine, 30th December, 1827

> The culture of Sugar Cane is becoming very general. Gen. Hernandez, who has a plantation thirty miles south of this place, calculates to plant nearly 300 acres the ensuing season. From 300 acres of cane, a clear profit of at least *twenty thousand dollars* may be made. This is far better than raising the finest of Sea Island Cotton.

Hernandez needed all the enslaved people he could get to make his $20,000. According to his contract with Smith he was to pay $2.00 each per month for "twenty African negroes from the wreck of the Spanish brig" from March 18, 1828 until February 1, 1829.

Hernandez was a deadbeat and never paid, and after using the Africans for labor for over 10 months he claimed in a lawsuit for payment brought by Smith that he didn't have to pay for their work because Smith had no right to make slaves of them. The outcome of the lawsuit is unclear, but it certainly seems to this historian that Hernandez had no elevated sentiments for the Africans but instead desired free labor. The plantation owners of Cuba certainly had their counterparts in Florida.

Hernandez' plantation was named Mala Compra (Spanish for "bad buy"). Today some land of the plantation is now Washington Oaks State Gardens, a beautiful place with a rose garden, azaleas and camellias, sandwiched between the surf of the Atlantic on one side and a river and marshes on the other. My first visit there was because of my botanical interest. I did not know then the sordid past of the place. My second visit was a far different experience. I could envision the Africans doing heavy labor there. The reflecting pools of the garden held my attention, because there was now much to reflect on.

One of the Africans died by accident the first month on Hernandez' plantation.[128] There is more on sickness and death in the group: on April 2nd Smith wrote, "Six have died since they were landed in Florida [at Key West], and thirteen are now sick, ten are on the recovery and three are dangerously ill."[129]

Smith's accounting in his suit of what Hernandez owed him reveals this: that three men escaped Hernandez' slavery for freedom in the wilderness of North Florida. They had been on the plantation for less than three months before they could not tolerate any more abuse. They stayed free men in the wilderness until May 12th of 1829, some 11 months later, when Waters Smith recorded "Cash paid Indians taking runaway Negroes $30.00."[130] Black men escaping from forced labor and terror on a continent 4,000 miles from home had been captured by the red man to be delivered to the white man, for money. This was probably a benevolent effort by Smith; he may have offered a reward especially so the Africans could be brought to him and transported back to their continent. But the Africans could not have known that. They may have even been living with the Indians, who brought them back to where they didn't want to be - the civilization of the white man.

To the south of the gardens is Bing's Landing Preserve, a county park. This was where Hernandez lived. Today archaeologist Ted M. Payne is finding the remains of his house and plantation buildings, destroyed 1835-1837 during Florida's Second Seminole War, a war which militia commander Hernandez fought in. He filed a war claim for the loss of his property afterward. In it is written the Hernandez home was "built of the best materials." Payne has even found where the housing for the enslaved people was.[131]

Historian Dr. Patricia C. Griffin working with Payne on this project has found a map of the plantation drawn in

1818, and several differing views of Hernandez' treatment of enslaved people. Two men, Matthew Long and James Pellicer - Pellicer had lived at Mala Compra - wrote they were

> Well acquainted with the Negroes upon the plantations; that they were industrious, had collected little comforts around them, which they had earned from cultivating and improving a small portion of ground, which they were allowed to have for their own individual benefit; that they appeared to be well off, if not better, than Negroes generally are.

Myer M. Cohen, an officer in the Seminole war wrote "the Negroes of General Hernandez...were singularly distinguished for their truth and fidelity to their owners."

Griffin found one other comment on Hernandez' treatment that contradicts the two above, by Theo Flotard and Venancio Sanchez, St. Augustine residents, on what happened to the enslaved on the Hernandez plantation after it was abandoned in the war. All of these references were not made in regard to the Africans on the plantation in 1828 and 1829, but were on those enslaved on the plantation in the mid 1830s:

> Negroes from St. Joseph's and Mala Compra, about eighty in number, of all ages, he [Hernandez] had to place them on the beach on the island of St. Anastasia; that he had some hired out in this city, and others at work on the public works, but the remainder have been kept on the island, employed in cutting stone and wood, but their hire and labor have not realized as much as was necessary for their support.

Historian Griffin adds this: that Dr. Samuel S. Peck attended to those on the island and he recorded that,

> In consequence of the removing of his Negroes from their comfortable homes, and their being placed on the island of St. Anastasia, without protection from the weather in the winter season, they became diseased, and many of them died; which the deponent believes was in consequence of such exposure..[132]

I asked Dr. Griffin about the character (or lack of character) of Joseph M. Hernandez. She replied,

> He was an opportunist for sure and maybe not even too scrupulous sometimes...For awhile ...he seemed to either use Spanish law or US law whichever suited his goals...He died with practically all of his Florida land holdings mortgaged as well as most of his slaves, also, did not always pay his overseers.[133]

Waters Smith submitted an accounting of the situation of the Africans in his custody about ten months after the wrecking of the *Guerrero*.[134] Eight of those months the Africans had spent in North Florida.

Statement showing the present situation of the Africans

[October 27, 1828, addressed to the Secretary of the Navy]

Received from Col. Wm. Pinkney Collector at Key West

121

From which number there died at Key West & St. Augustine

9

The Interpreter included in the original number, not being
one of the slave cargo, was discharged by order of
Judge [of the US District Court Joseph Lee] Smith

1

Now in custody   111

Of this number there are sick and blind which are
supported at a small expense

10

Boys for whom no wages are received

9

Men not able to do much work, no wages exacted

3

Hired at Two dollars per month, to be cloathed by me

89

111

Two dollars per month may appear low wages for the Negroes hired out;
but when it is taken into consideration that these Negroes had never been
used to work, and that two or three years are required to learn Africans to
be of much service on a plantation it will be seen that it is fair wages for
the first year. The above disposition was made of them in the course of
the month of April last; the wages due on the first of March next for the
89 will be about $1,780
which will form an item of credit to the Government on the settlement of
my accounts.

Respectfully submitted by Your Most Obedient Servant,
Waters Smith

Chapter Eleven

Washington, D. C.
1828 - 1829

Inadequate Response in the Capital

The Africans were in a legal no place, for they had landed *accidentally* in US territory and therefore America's anti-slave trade laws, which addressed *importation*, were not adequate to cover their situation. President Adams' diary has these entries made in April, 1828. The first is on a visit by Secretary of the Navy Southard and Attorney General William Wirt:

> Mr. Southard and Mr. Wirt came together and presented a question upon the Act of Congress of 1819 for the suppression of the slave trade, which involves the legality of all executive proceedings in the case of the Africans lately landed at Key West from the stranded Spanish vessel, fleeing from the pursuit of a British armed vessel and who have since been transferred to St. Augustine in Florida. The Act of 3 March 1819 is a penal statute, all the provisions of which are directed against citizens or residents of the United States participating in that traffic or against an unlawful introduction of slaves into the United States. In this case the Africans were landed from the wreck of a foreign vessel to save their lives. No unlawful attempt was made to introduce them into the

United States - no citizen or resident of the United States appears to have had any concern in the transactions, so far as the slave trade was intended by it, and the provisions of this law do in no respect apply to it....We concluded that it would be necessary to propose a supplementary Act of Congress.

Later in the month the President wrote:

There was a short cabinet meeting at one o'clock, the result of which was a determination that a message should be sent to Congress....I desired Mr. [Richard] Rush to send me copies of the papers relating to the Negroes landed at Key West from the stranded Spanish prize ship and since transferred to Saint Augustine. These papers it will be necessary to send to Congress with the message.[135]

His message was delivered April 30, 1828:

In the month of December last, one hundred and twenty-one African negroes were landed at Key West from a Spanish slave-trading vessel, stranded within the jurisdiction of the United States, while pursued by an armed schooner in his Britannic Majesty's service. The Collector of the Customs at Key West took possession of these persons, who were afterwards delivered over to the Marshal of the Territory of East Florida, by whom they were conveyed to St. Augustine, where they still remain.

Believing that the circumstances under which they have been cast upon the compassion of the country, are not embraced by the provisions of the act of Congress of 3d March, 1819, or of the other acts prohibiting the Slave Trade, I submit, to the consideration of Congress, the expediency of a supplementary act, directing and authorizing such measures as may be necessary for removing them from the territory of the United States, and for fulfilling towards them the obligations of humanity.

John Quincy Adams[136]

Besides the *Guerrero* people Adams also became involved in the plight of the Cuban coastal slave ship *Amistad*'s Africans much later, in the 1840s. He is described by historian Howard Jones in his book *Mutiny on the Amistad* as not an abolitionist, but still he hated slavery as inhumane and conflicting to the Declaration of Independence.[137]

But Adams' effort was not enough. The President's message was referred to the Committee on the Judiciary. What happened - or didn't happen - there has not been discovered.

Waters Smith asked for reimbursement of his expenses on April 2nd, in a letter to Secretary Rush. He had paid $3,000 for care and transport of the Africans and "I am not in a situation to lay out of so large a sum without serious inconvenience." He asked for an advance of $4,000 and related that he had been bonded to the US for $20,000 and $10,000 with security given in his position as US Marshal. "Government will therefore hazard nothing by making the advance," he wrote. He was told the matter would be under the direction of the Secretary of the Navy, Samuel L. Southard.

On July 16, 1828, Smith had written Southard on the problem with Lewis, the African interpreter.

The Navy Secretary's reply was a non-reply, "It is

not thought proper under the circumstances for this Dept. to give any order respecting Lewis." Smith, a former lawyer, wanted the law behind any of his actions, and took the matter of Lewis to US District Court Judge Joseph Lee Smith, who ordered Lewis released. His son, however, remained with the group, according to the October 27, 1828 accounting.

In response to Smith's plea to be reimbursed, Southard wrote:

> The case of these negroes was presented to Congress by a message of the President during the last session but no [financial] provision was made to dispose of them. No instructions will therefore be given at present for sending them out of the Country. The best disposition must be made of them, so that they may occasion the least possible expense. They can no doubt, as in other cases, support themselves & you will take such measures by hiring them out...[138]

But Smith had already done that! And his expenses continued, as he had agreed to pay for the Africans' clothing and there were sick and blind men placed at an expense under the care of Francis J. Ross. Ross was a Justice of the Peace who lived near Jacksonville, and must have been well trusted by Waters Smith to care for these men.

On the same day Smith had written to Rush on his expenses he had also sent a copy of his letter with the story of his financial outlays for the Africans to Florida Delegate to Congress Joseph M. White; "I think you can aid me," he wrote.[139]

The summer passed. On October 27th Smith again wrote a letter - a long one - to Southard, and, coming from nearby Baltimore where he purchased winter clothing for the Africans, was in Washington to deliver it in person. By then he had paid for the transportation of the Africans from Key West and partially supported them with thousands of dollars of his own money since the previous December.

President Adams recorded in his diary that he met with Southard October 28th over Smith's claim, and the next day with District Attorney Daniel Brent on the same subject and finally, on October 31st, with Waters Smith. The President told Smith that no appropriation had been made for his expenses.

Smith wrote Southard the next day. "I have seen the President on the subject of the Africans...I am perfectly satisfied that it is a case in which neither yourself or the President, under the existing laws can afford me relief." He asked that Southard formally reply to his October 27 letter and the President's decision, for "the future progress of this business....I leave this city early on Monday for Florida."[140]

On November 5th Southard saw Adams on Smith's claim again, and on November 18th wrote Smith a curt letter:

> Your letters of the 27th ult. [ultimo - last month] and 1st instant have been received and submitted to the consideration of the President of the US. I am instructed by him to inform you, that there is no appropriation nor any fund, out of which payment of the expense you claim can be satisfied.
>
> It is not intended by this general answer to express any opinion in favor of the correctness and justice of your accounts; there seem to be objections to them, which would be investigated if the authority to settle and pay them existed; one among these objections is the smallness of the sum for which the Africans are hired out.[141]

It seems some conscience set in with Southard after he mailed that letter, a letter that doomed the futures of Smith and of the Africans, for two days later Southard wrote to John Hanson, who perhaps was a member of the American

Colonization Society, in Philadelphia, "Be pleased to inform me whether you intend sending a vessel to Cape Mesurado shortly, or if you know of any one bound there."[142] Cape Mesurado was a nearly 300' geographical feature on the Liberian coast, where Monrovia had been founded.

A week later Southard wrote in his Report to Congress that Smith had been advised to hire the Africans out and "It is presumed he has done so." Southard *knew* Smith had hired them out. He wrote that the Africans did not come under the (anti-slave trade) law

> That entrusts this department with the direction and control of Africans brought within our jurisdiction and direct them to be sent to the agency on the coast of Africa....[I] do not feel authorized to devote to this object any portion of the money appropriated for the suppression of the slave trade.

What perplexities Southard had about including the situation of the *Guerrero* Africans into the funds he had for returning rescued Africans to Africa at Liberia were not revealed, but he did end his report in favor of doing *something* about the situation (which was the opposite position he seemed to take in his letter to Smith nine days earlier). His report continued:

> It is important that some authority be given by law to dispose of these Africans and settle the accounts of the marshal.[143]

The Africans continued to labor on the plantations of North Florida. On January 13, 1829 a resolution was offered by Representative Clement Dorsey (Md.) for the Committee on Naval Affairs to report on making provision by law "for removing from the territory of the US certain African negroes landed at Key West." It was ordered to "lay on the table."[144]

Eleven days later Southard wrote to US Agent at Liberia Dr. Richard Randall that it was probable that "from 100 to 110 Africans" would be sent there "in a few weeks."[145] On March 3rd Southard left his position as Secretary of the Navy, and was replaced by John Branch. Waters Smith's efforts had to start nearly all over again - with someone even more difficult than Southard had been.

On March 29, 1829 Congress voted $16,000 for the expenses of Waters Smith and to transport the Africans to Liberia. Delegate White informed Smith of the vote, which White may have fostered.

On April 22nd Smith wrote to John Branch, explaining Southard's refusal to pay his expenses but with the $16,000 appropriation then law, asked instructions on whether he should forward his account and vouchers or bring them himself to Washington "that a settlement may be had." He requested $6,000-$8,000 with a much larger sum due, but that the sum requested "will relieve me from the pressure which I have long felt." He included a copy of his $20,000 bond that was in the hands of the Comptroller of the Treasury. A condition of the bond was "to account for all monies which may come into my hands: I name this to show that the Government will be perfectly secure in remitting to me the sum required."[146]

Branch started right in on what seems to me to be the trivial pursuits of rich men in power, to toy with a decent, honest, small-town underling in distant Florida:

May 8, 1829

I have received your letter of the 22nd ult. requesting a remittance on account of your claims for supporting certain Africans and before any remittance can be made, it is necessary that you should provide satisfactory evidence of the justice of the claim.

John Branch[147]

Although Branch wouldn't part with a dime for Smith he did begin work to get the Africans to Africa with part of the $16,000. Although that sum was allocated March 2nd, it took until June 5th until he began writing letters of inquiry on the chartering of a private vessel to make the voyage to Cape Mesurado. In the three months he did nothing Branch, a future Florida plantation owner, apparently did not concern himself with what the Africans' situation was; legally free people under an overseer's whip in North Florida.

Branch wrote June 15th to Smith that John McPhail of Norfolk would transport the Africans, and Smith should prepare to embark them on August 1st.

His instructions to McPhail of the same date, given through the Navy agent at Norfolk were, conversely, kindly towards the Africans, stipulating that there should be "sufficient and comfortable accommodation, good and wholesome provisions and water and kind treatment on the passage...everything necessary for their comfort and sustenance during the voyage." McPhail would be paid $26 for those over 10 years of age, $10 for those under that age, less than he had been paid for a similar voyage in 1827.[148]

At the same time Branch wrote to Dr. Randall at Cape Mesurado, to expect the Africans.

On June 27th Branch advised Smith that A. Hamilton Mechlin of Washington would superintend the transportation of the Africans to Africa and would be accompanied by Dr. John Vaughn Smith, US Navy doctor, and that McPhail's *Nautilus* would sail from Norfolk on July 3rd.

But Smith was not in St. Augustine to receive that letter - he had come to Washington apparently to see the President again. Branch wrote instructions to Smith while he was there on July 1st, "In obedience to the orders of the President of the United States dated yesterday - you are to immediately proceed from here to St. Augustine" to prepare the embarkation of the Africans onboard a ship bound to Liberia.

The next day Branch's arrangements began to fall apart. First, the voyage was postponed for three weeks partially because of a request by the American Colonization Society. At the end of the month the *Nautilus* was declared unseaworthy, so Branch then made an agreement with the owner of a Boston ship, William Ropes, who then changed his mind about the voyage and suggested a New York and Norfolk vessel, the *Washington's Barge*. Her owner, Richard Churchward of New York, offered the Navy better terms, anyway. On August 11th Branch wrote to the Navy Yard in Norfolk on provisions to be placed aboard and that "the departure is to be expedited."

Dr. Smith and A. Hamilton Mechlin were to meet in Baltimore and receive nine Africans into their care there. Two were brought from Mobile and were in the custody of the Baltimore marshal, as was one who was left with him by a Baltimore resident who was about to leave the US. Also six Kroomen from a South American privateer, the *William Tell*, who were with the Collector of Customs in Baltimore, would join the group.

Kroomen were from a tribe, the Kru, that lived just south of Cape Mesurado. Because there was no harbor on the coast they had developed specialized skills as seamen to bring ship passengers in their boats over the surf to land. They carried notebooks with them as to their service to various captains, and proudly noted that they would never be enslaved, and then, worked both sides of the slave trade, for both the slave traders and for the Navy cruisers patrolling for them. And, indeed, they were so valuable to operations that the slavers did not enslave them, and they worked all along the West Coast of Africa. They were identified by an inch-wide dark blue tattoo than ran from the hairline to the end of the nose.

One of the Africans refused to go, the two from Mobile escaped from Mechlin at Norfolk, so, after provisioning of the vessel at Norfolk Mechlin, Dr. Smith, and the six Kroomen sailed in the *Washington's Barge*, Capt. A. H. Wing, for North Florida. Smith had told Branch that Fernandina, Amelia Island, would be more convenient to embark from than St. Augustine, to the south of there.

Chapter Twelve

September, 1829
Amelia Island, Florida

Return to Africa

Amelia Island today is known for very expensive homes and a golf course on the beach but not particularly for its rich history unless one wants to include Victorian houses and Florida's oldest operating saloon (which, by the way, serves a great Margarita). But some of the past human drama of this place is evident in a 1600s Spanish mission site, of massive Ft. Clinch, begun in 1847, an 1839 lighthouse, a beach for African-Americans in the segregation era now preserved, and, "Old Town" - the original site of Fernandina.

In 1811, when Florida was still owned by Spain (that country ceded Florida to the US effective in 1821), Spanish Governor Enrique White ordered that the town be organized into regular plots, straight streets, with a central plaza on the Amelia River. It was certainly an ironic place to leave from for freedom in Africa. The port had been a refuge adjacent to the old US border at Georgia for privateers and their prizes, many of which were slave ships captured in the Straits of Florida coming from Africa. The Africans aboard would from there be smuggled into the United States. Belton A. Copp, writing from the area to John Quincy Adams, then Secretary of State, in 1818, on the slave traders declared:

> Nothing could have caused these people to become more depraved than they now manifest themselves to be. But this traffic in

human blood they are unwilling to relinquish, tis so profitable a business.[149]

That same year the privateers brought in two human cargoes, "in such a condition of misery from long confinement, starvation, and scourging [whipping]," it was noted in a later case on the slave trade, "that the representation of it caused all over the United States a deep and indignant sympathy."[150]

In part because of the scandalous activities at Amelia Island, wrote slave trade historian Hugh Thomas, new anti-slave trading acts were passed by Congress in 1818, 1819, and 1820.[151] The next year Fernandina became American. The town was described that year by James Forbes:

> The town consists of about forty houses, built of wood, in six streets, regularly intersecting each other at right angles, having rows of trees (Pride of India) and a square, with a small fort of eight guns, fronting the water. Several of these houses are two stories high, with galleries, and form a handsome appearance.

A Spanish fort, Fort San Carlos, was on a bluff overlooking the river. It was built mostly of wood and earth, and all traces of it except for a brick footing have disappeared. Then a railroad was built, and the entire town of Fernandina moved to its present location - where the Victorian houses and the oldest saloon with the Margarita are - because of the railroad. The original site of Fernandina then became known as "Old Town." It was there - the original Fernandina - that Kingsley had purchased a lot in 1811 to build a warehouse,[152] no doubt for his agricultural business. It possibly was used to house the 100 Africans who awaited the arrival of the *Washington's Barge.*

Waters Smith to John Branch

Fernandina, Amelia Island
Florida 21 August 1829

Sir

I arrived here on the morning of the 16
Instant, with the greatest part of the Africans:
but the Brig *Nautilus* has not yet made her
appearance: I have all the Africans ready for
embarcation with the exception of five: one
of this number was with Capt. Doane, whose
bond I hold for the delivery of the boy when
called for, under the penalty of $500. Capt.
Doane is now absent he has the boy with him,
and is not expected to be in Florida until
October next; this is contrary to my
agreement with him. One other was left on the
Plantation of Francis J. Ross Esq. on St. Johns
River; I had placed with Mr. Ross nine sick
men; one died before my return from
Washington; and when my deputy called for
the remaining eight, one was so ill as to
render it improper to remove him, on the
arrival of the brig, it is my intention to request
the surgeon, to visit the negro, if he is still
living, and be governed by the opinion of the
surgeon as to his removal. The other three
absenties, are part of the 36 hired to Z.
Kingsley Esq. As soon as possible after my
arrival at St. Augustine (which was the 4th
Instant) I notified all there who had Africans
in possession, of the order I had received to
have them in readiness at Fernandina on the
15 Instant for embarcation; Mr. Kingsley with
others was notified on receipt of my letter he
came immediately to St. Augustine to see me,

and arrangements were made; apparently to his entire satisfaction for the delivery of the 36 Africans in his possession: The day following was ____[illegible] for our leaving town for that purpose: There are a few persons in St. Augustine, who have been actively, but secretly engaged ever since my return from Washington, in throwing every obstacle in the way of the execution of your order. I shall consider it my duty in a future communication, to give an more particular account of this business; at present I by leave state that Mr. Kingsley was so far _____[ill.] on, as to change his mind, and determine not to deliver the Africans in his possession: He informed me, that he had the written opinion of John Rodman Esq. Collector of the Customs for St. Augustine which opinion was sustained by still higher authority; stating That there was no law, authorising the Secretary of the Navy or the President of the U. States to order the Africans to be sent out of Florida, that they were free men, and could not be sent to Africa contrary to their wishes, and that the marshal had no legal authority to take them from the possession of Mr. Kingsley and others. I will endeavour to procure a copy of this legal opinion, and forward to you.

Partly by force and partly by persuasion I have obtained from Mr. Kingsley 33 of the 36 Africans which were in his possession. A boat which I sent to his plantation for the remaining 3, has just returned without them the overseer stating, that they have run away, and could not be found: I am satisfied they could be found in three hours, if the necessary order was given by Mr. Kingsley: I still think that I shall get them, as I will go myself to the plantation for that purpose. I should have gone in the boat which has just returned, but, that for two or three days there has been some suspicious characters from Georgia, lurking about the town, I think with intention of stealing some of these Africans if an opportunity offers. This compels me to keep a guard and for myself constantly on the elert - They have done no act which will authorize me to arrest them, I can therefore only keep a watch on them. I shall be unpleasantly situate until the arrival of the Brig to take the Africans on board.

Capt. Stotesbury of the St. Marys revenue cutter has offered his services to aid me in protecting the Africans; and has been 24 hours anchored in the harbor to prevent the departure of any boat without examination.[133]

Smith refers twice to men (the first reference made in regard to Key West) who would steal the free Africans and force them into slavery. His was not an overactive imagination at work; it happened regularly.[154]

A week later Marshal Smith again wrote to John Branch, that he had obtained the three men from the Kingsley Plantation and all Africans with the exception of the one with Capt. Doane were now gathered and ready to embark. Yet the *Washington's Barge* (Smith was still expecting the *Nautilus*, not being informed otherwise) which should have been there by then, due to the prevailing winds of the past two weeks, was not. This delay, he wrote, was causing considerable expense and inconvenience to him. Yet Waters Smith again showed his true concern for the Africans' welfare when he wrote on August 28th:

Business requires my personal attention in other parts of my district; still I cannot with safety leave...until the Africans are on board the vessel, and I find it prudent and necessary, still, to continue a guard at night.

He wrote he would stay at Fernandina until Sept. 4th, then move the Africans to a more secure place, "at less expence than at this place," but where they can be delivered within 10 days after the brig's arrival, so as not to subject the government to the expense of demurrage.[155]

On September 2nd the *Washington's Barge* sailed past Amelia Island to St. Augustine to disembark passengers Thomson Mason and family. That was Capt. Wing's orders from the owner, Richard Churchward. The St. Augustine newspaper announced the ship's arrival, in the same edition where several "Marshal's Sale" of property were advertised. Two of them are sad and converse, for Waters Smith would, in front of the court house on December 1st, by order of the Superior Court for the Eastern District of Florida sell "one negro woman named Caty, taken as the property of Antonio P. Medicis, administrix of Francis de Medicis deceased at their suit of Jos. S. Sanchez, Executor of Joseph Sanchez, deceased" and on the same day also sell, "two negro men, taken as the property of Lewis and Sophia Fleming at the suit of Andrew Low - Terms of sale, cash."[156]

What is even more converse is that Smith himself was a slave owner. In the 1830 census of St. Augustine is found that living at his family home just south of the massive stone fortress were Waters and his wife Mary and six children, also two enslaved males and seven enslaved females, three of the females being children under 10 years old. And, a "free colored male" whose age fell into the 24-36 census category also was part of the household.[157]

The *Washington's Barge* could not sail northward back to Amelia Island because of adverse winds, for weeks, until September 27th, an excruciating wait for Smith. In the meantime Secretary of the US Navy, John Branch, decided to concentrate on things like raisans, firing off a letter to Commander James Barron of the Norfolk Navy Yard on the provisioning of the *Washington's Barge*: "wine, chocolate, tea, pickles, salt, raisans" were "unnecessary to be entered under the head of Hospital Stores, and extravagant in price." Branch wanted from Barron "an explanation of the circumstances or reasons, which induced you to sanction the accounts with your signature."[158]

On September 30, 1829 the *Washington's Barge* with 100 recaptured Africans and six Kroomen aboard sailed for Liberia. In the year 1830 enslaved in the United States were 2,000,000 people. The Africans from the slave ship *Guerrero* were not then part of that number.

Two boys were left behind, for Dr. Smith determined they had the highly contagious disease yaws. Yaws is caused by a bacteria similar to syphilis, but is not sexually transmitted. It can enter the body through cut skin in hot, humid areas from contact with the huge sores of others infected with yaws. It destroys tissue and bone, and today can be cured with a single shot of penicillin. The latent period, the time between the time the bacteria enters the body and the appearance of the symptoms is 7-8 weeks.[159] The boys had not been infected on the slave ship, nor in Key West, but were infected in the terrible conditions in which they lived on the plantations of North Florida.

And yaws only affects children under the age of 15 - evidence that Gomez had taken many young people, for they had been by that time almost two years in Florida, and, because of their contagion, were not the (apparently) very very young boys Smith had placed with St. Augustine families that did not have to work.

Branch wrote Waters Smith on October 30th, a month after the *Washington's Barge* had sailed, that he had received his account and vouchers and they were sent to the auditor for settlement. He wrote Smith with the same attitude he had written Commander Barron with over the raisans:

From the extravagant and doubtful character of some of the charges, and slight evidence in support of them, they deserve his [the auditor's] usual vigilance and rigid scrutiny in adjusting them.[160]

On December 9th Waters Smith was reimbursed far, far less than his expenses were. He received $4,208.32.[161] The following July Smith mortgaged his house - to Zephaniah Kingsley.[162]

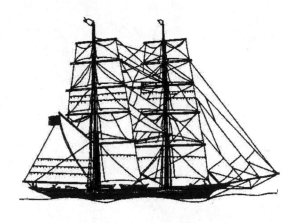

Ship Designs
Representative of what the *Guerrero*, a brig (top)
and HBM *Nimble*, a schooner (bottom) may have looked like.

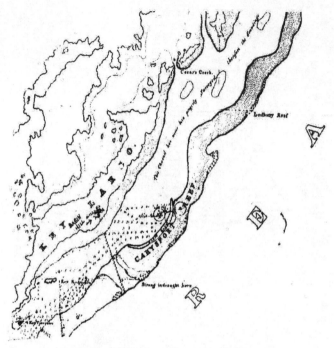

1838 "Chart of the Great Florida Reef"

This chart shows Bason Bank (spelled here "Basin") where the lightship was moored, Key Tavernier, where there was a wreckers' station, Key Largo, Carysfort Reef, and Black Caesar's Creek (written here Cesar's Creek) where the *Thorn* and *Surprize* were anchored. The circles indicate where a lighthouse could be best built.

Secretaries of the Navy Samuel Southard (l.) and John Branch (r.)

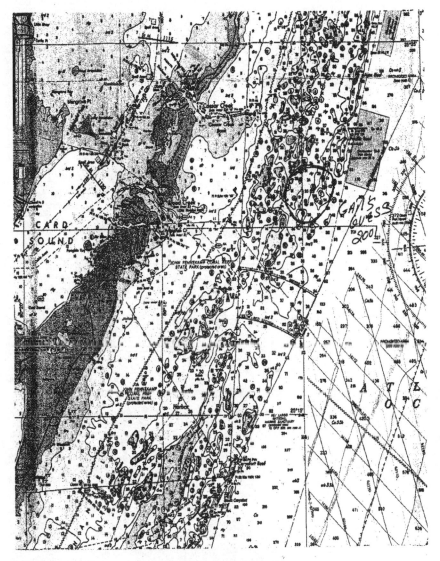

The Upper Florida Keys
This chart shows Basin Hill Shoals, Turtle Harbor, Key Largo,
Pacific Reef, and Caesar Creek, with "Gail's Guess 2001" as
for the probable location of the wreck of the *Guerrero*.

Log of HBM *Nimble*, December 19, 1827
(London. Public Record Office ADM1/3322.)

Key West in 1826

Sketch by famed naturalist Titian Ramsay Peale

Top of drawing "Key West" and bottom of drawing,
"Allertown from the Commodores house looking north"

The departure of the "Guerrero" was reported in our Despatch No. 32 of 1827, and it is there stated that she was well armed, and had a crew of ninety men; and that her probable intention was to plunder of their cargoes of slaves, any weaker vessels that she might fall in with on the coast of Africa. We understand that she carried her intention fully into effect, and that she not only plundered slave vessels, but some other Merchant ships; and accordingly at the time of her capture and loss she had a valuable Cargo of European Merchandize on board.

Pirate Ship
Kilbee and Macleay's dispatch to London verifying the piratical attacks of the *Guerrero*.

(London. Public Record Office. FO 84/80, p. 18, no. 3)

Former Governor John Geddes Residence in Charleston

On the far right is 122 Meeting St., where Geddes lived when the wreckers solicited his
help for payment by the British for saving HBM *Nimble*. Geddes and Charles Edmonston
wrote on their behalf to Secretary of State Henry Clay. Geddes died two months later.
This house burned in the 1861 fire.

(South Carolina Historical Society)

**President John Quincy Adams,
his diary entry on the
"Negroes Landed at Key West"
and his Message to Congress on
"fulfilling towards them the
obligations of humanity"**

To the Senate and House of Representatives of the United States:

WASHINGTON, 30th April, 1822.

In the month of December last, one hundred and twenty-one African negroes were landed at Key West from a Spanish slave-trading vessel, stranded within the jurisdiction of the United States, while pursued by an armed schooner in his Britannic Majesty's service. The Collector of the Customs at Key West took possession of these persons, who were afterwards delivered over to the Marshal of the Territory of East Florida, by whom they were conveyed to St. Augustine, where they still remain.

Believing that the circumstances under which they have been cast upon the compassion of the country, are not embraced by the provisions of the act of Congress of 3d March, 1819, or of the other acts prohibiting the Slave Trade, I submit, to the consideration of Congress, the expediency of a supplementary act, directing and authorizing such measures as may be necessary for removing them from the territory of the United States, and for fulfilling towards them the obligations of humanity.

JOHN QUINCY ADAMS,

for removing Blacks is, That after having brought up the large arrears of his debts to the government, he has now fallen afresh into delinquency — There was a short Cabinet Meeting at one O'clock, the result of which was a determination that a Message should be sent to Congress recommending a supplementary act to that of 3. March 1819, authorizing the President of the United States to send to Africa, negroes taken, from vessels of the United States unlawfully engaged in the Slave trade — The question was unanimous that the law as now existing limits the Power of the President to the disposal of persons imported into the United States in violation of the laws against the Slave Trade — I desired M. Rush to send me copies of the papers relating to the Negroes landed at Key West from the stranded Spanish Prize Ships and since transferred to Saint Augustine — These papers at

(National Archives)

AFRICANS AT KEY WEST.

MESSAGE

FROM THE

PRESIDENT OF THE UNITED STATES,

RELATIVE TO THE DISPOSITION OF

THE AFRICANS LANDED AT KEY WEST

FROM A

STRANDED SPANISH VESSEL.

APRIL 30, 1828.

Read, and referred to the Committee on the Judiciary.

WASHINGTON :

PRINTED BY GALES & SEATON.

1828.

MANIFEST *of the whole Cargo on board the Schooner General Geddes, John Morrison master, burthen seventy-seven tons, bound from Key West for St. Augustine.*

Marks & Number.	Number of Entries.	Packages & Contents.	Shippers.	Residence.	Consignees.	Residence.
		One hundred and fourteen Africans.	Waters Smith.	St. Augustine.	Waters Smith.	St. Augustine.

Manifest

This was included in the papers Deputy Collector of St. Augustine Thomas F. Cornell submitted for a claim for bounty.

(National Archives)

Zephaniah Kingsley Plantation House, post-Civil War era

Kingsley told Marshal Smith that the St. Augustine Collector of Customs told him there was no law made in Washington for the Africans to be sent to Africa and refused to turn over the 36 Africans at work on his plantation. Smith wrote to the Secretary of the Navy, "Partly by force and partly by persuasion I have obtained [them]."

(Photo collection of the National Park Service)

Ruins of Hernandez' *Mala Compra* Plantation

Located at Bing's Landing County Park, 30 miles south of St. Augustine, the buildings were destroyed in the Second Seminole War. One of the Africans died at *Mala Compra*.

(Photo by the author, 2004)

Old Slave Houses at the Kingsley Plantation, Fort George Island, North Florida, 1870s

(Harpers New Monthly Magazine.)

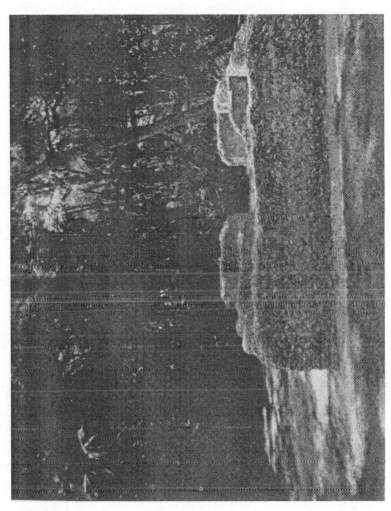

Ruins of one of the Slave Houses (which were already built when the Africans arrived), 1990s

(Photo by the Author.)

Joseph M. Hernandez

Hernandez claimed in response to Marshal Waters Smith's lawsuit for payment that the Africans were not slaves, therefore he didn't have to pay for their hire. Yet that story came after he labored them 10 months on his plantation, where three of the Africans ran away.

(Florida State Archives.)

Genr. Joseph M. Hernandez

1828   To Waters Smith Marshal — Dr

April 18 To hire of 19 Africans due this day as $ Bond... $38.—
                    Intt. to 18 April 1830 @ 6$8c ... 4.56 $42.56

May 18   " do ...19 ... do ....3 same ....38.—
                         Interest do .... 4.37 ... 42.37

June 18   " do ...19 ... do ... $38.— Interest $4.13 .... 42.18

July 18   " do ...16 ... do ....32.. ... $ .. 3.38 .... 35.38

August 18 " do ...16 ... do ....32 ... $ ..3.20 ....35.20

Septem 18 " do ...16 ... do ....32 ... $ ..3.4 .... 35.4

October 18 " do ...16 ... do ....32 ... $ ..2.88 ....34.88

November 18 " do ...16 ... do ...32 ... $ ..2.72 ..... 34.72

December 18 " do ...16 ... do ...32 ... $ ..2.56 ..... 34.56

1829
January 18 " do ...16 ... do ...32 ... $ ..2.40 ..... 34.40

           " do ...16 for 17 days ...18.18 ... $ ...1.27 ... 18.42
February 4

May 12   " Cash paid Indians taking runaway Negroes ... $30.— $339.71
           " Interest from 12 May 1829 to 18 April 1830 . ... 1.63   31.63

           Interest on $386 15/100 / being the amount of the $421.39
           above account of Interest from the   1.93
           18 April 1830 to the 17 May 1830 . ...
                                                     $423.32

Marshal Waters Smith vs. Joseph M. Hernandez, 1830:
Accounting of Sums Due for Hire of the Africans;
May 12, 1829, "Cash paid Indians taking runaway Negroes $ 30."

(St. Johns County, Florida Court Records, Box 166, File 76)

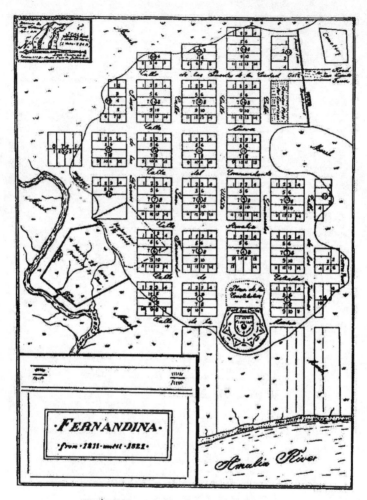

Plat of Fernandina, Amelia Island

The plat shows a location owned by Kingsley since 1811 when he intended on building a warehouse. If it was indeed built it may have been rented to Marshal Smith as quarters for the Africans for the many days they waited for the arrival of the ship for Liberia. It is Lot 5, Square 18, to the left of *Paseo de las Damas* (now Ladies Street) between *Calle Amalia* (now Amelia Street) and *Calle del Commandante* (now Commandant Street). Notice too the then-existing Fort San Carlos next to the plaza. The plaza area still exists.

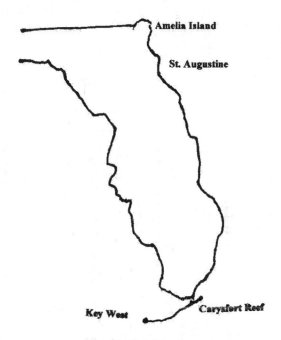

Florida Peninsula

(Above: Sketch by the author; Below: Photograph by the author, 2004)

Site of Fort San Carlos, Amelia Island
This is where the *Washington's Barge* would have sailed from for Liberia.
Only a footing (straight line in center of photograph) remains.

Barbados Governor James Lyon's Compliment to the Americans

"I am happy to have it in my power to bear testimony to the very assiduous care and attention shown by yourself and Dr. Smith to the comfort and welfare of the unfortunate Africans since the arrival of the vessel in Carlisle bay and with every wish for the prosperous termination of your labour."

Africa

(Sketch by the author)

Chapter Thirteen

December, 1829
Carlisle Bay, Barbados

In Terrible Distress

In paraphrasing documents historians often unknowingly - and sometimes, unfortunately, knowingly - put a "spin" on the facts. If I felt that the reader can get through the old and difficult English usage then I let the people of the 1820s and 1830s speak. That is why there are so very many quotes from the documents in this book.

In that light, here is another quote; excerpts from a letter by one who was in great distress, at having left North Florida for Liberia and ending up in Barbados, the appointed superintendent of the Africans, A. Hamilton Mechlin.

He wrote to His Excellency Sir James Lyon, Governor of Barbados, from "On Board the *Washington's Barge*," December 31, 1829:

> The American schooner *Washington's Barge* arrived in this port on the 27th inst. having on board ninety-five recaptured Africans embarked by the United States at Fernandina on Amelia Island and bound to the U. States' settlement of Cape Mesurado on the coast of Africa.

There had been 100 recaptured Africans aboard (that number does not include the Kru Africans) when the *Washington's Barge* left Amelia Island. Five, apparently, had already perished on the lengthy, interrupted voyage.

Mechlin continued:

> As Agent for the transportation of these
> Africans and being conscious that the British
> West India islands are closed to Americans I
> feel it a duty both to the authorities here and
> to those unfortunate Africans intrusted to my
> charge to detail to your Excellency the
> circumstances and causes that led to the
> entrance of the above named vessel into this
> harbor and to request most respectfully your
> Excellency's advice and assistance thereon.
> The Africans were recaptured by the U. States
> from a Spanish brig which ran ashore being
> pursued by a British man of war at Key
> West...

Since Americans were the victors in the
Revolutionary War the British punished them by restricting
and/or barring American trade in her West Indies
possessions. At this time American ships were totally barred
from British ports.

Briefly Mechlin told of the ordeal of the people, as
far as he knew it. Then, on to their ordeal at sea. His
narrative is confusing as to exactly where the *Washington's
Barge* sailed for 88 days, and some of the words could not be
determined. (I have represented those with blanks and/or
question marks.) It is quite obvious that Mechlin was totally
disgusted. The underlining is his:

> On the 30th September 1829 the Africans
> embarked and the schooner sailed for her port
> of destination. For upwards of a month
> subsequently she encountered a series of
> heavy gales and winds in which the mainmast
> and other spars were sprung - jib boom
> carried away the vessel aleak and other
> injuries done to the rigging yet still we might

have reached Cape Mesurado with ease and in safety had not the master and captain of the schooner been perfectly unfit from his consummate ignorance of navigation and seamanship to take charge of such a voyage as he has attempted.

To prove this it will be only necessary to state that before he had attempted in that meridian of longitude which it is customary and in fact necessary that navigators from America to that part of the Coast of Africa where Cape Mesurado is situated should reach over to make their ports of destination he ran south into the trade winds where the vessel must beat against a continual & strong head wind to gain her port. When in the latitude of the Cape Verd islands he judged himself to the East of them, and when in the latitude of Cape Mesurado to be within twenty four hours sail of his port whereas subsequent facts (which I will state) prove that _____ never was at any time, and at the ____ calculation less than six hundred miles west of the Verd islands, no less than fourteen hundred miles west of Cape Mesurado. On arriving in latitude of Cape Mesurado he endeavored upwards of four ____ beatings to reach the Coast of Africa but without success. He then determined to run North and Easterly in order either to make the coast of Africa or the Verd Islands and procure the necessary supplies - as our provisions and water were getting low - the vessel aleak and in want of ballast. But when in the latitude of said island and after running down latitude before the wind a distance greater than from the islands ____ Coast of Africa we concluded ourselves to be the leeward of ___ and were obliged to continue on to the nearest of the West India Islands, Barbados, where we fortunately arrived on the 27th. The distance ran by the *Washington's Barge* calculated by ___ since___she bore away before the wind to this island, is ___ teen hundred miles. The distance from the Cape Verd Islands to Barbados is more than twenty one hundred miles, and the distance of Cape Mesurado to Barbados is about three thousand miles. The ____ must have been six hundred miles west of the Verd islands over fourteen hundred in the same [?] direction from his [?] port [?] being at that time more than two months at sea without seeing _____. I am thus tediously particular on this point, because I can ___ in the captain's ignorance the cause of the vessel not reaching her destination, of her being altogether eighty eight days at sea without seeing land, finally of her entrance into this port in distress - and I should very unwilling to commit my own, or the lives of those entrusted to my charge again to another voyage across the Atlantic under his _____.

Besides being storm tossed and lost with damaged masts the vessel's old water casks had burst. Mechlin later wrote to John Branch: "The water was lost and had it not been for the rain water caught we should all immediately have perished." The night after they made port in Carlisle Bay, Barbados, two of the Africans, not being stopped by a crew who were in a "mutinous state" with "no water left" stole the vessel's boat and headed for shore. Mechlin had a Barbadian officer apprehend them and then set a guard at night - the six Kroomen, whom Mechlin paid, "not only to prevent a recurrance...but to keep all boats off at night lest some [of the Africans] should [be] kidnapped" and sold into slavery in Barbados! Three times had kidnapping been attempted or feared - at Key West, at Fernandina, and then at Barbados. The black man, kidnapped from his home in Africa, faced even more kidnappings in the New World. It was a terrible time.

Mechlin then presented his case to the Governor and members of his council in person, showing his papers that read that the ship's name was supposed to be the *Nautilus* and it was supposed to have departed from *St. Augustine*, but Waters Smith had convinced Branch that Fernandina would be better. Both of those names had changed verbally, but not on paper. Mechlin wrote to Branch the Barbadians "declared (and I think with reason) that the entry of the negroes into a port so far out of their way" and the name changes "were (very) very suspicious circumstances."

But Mechlin was believed, after a survey of the *Washington's Barge* was done. This is the surveyors' report to the Governor:

> That in the present state of the vessel as she now lies in Carlisle Bay she is not fit to proceed on her voyage without being hove out in the careenage and thoroughly caulked all over & cleaned inside - we find her main mast sprung near the partners - her fore stay carried away - jibboom stove and main top mast sprung, fore top sail yard sprung - her masts too long and recommend them to be considerably shortened - her sails to be overhauled and repaired - her water casks coopered and added to and being ___[illegible] completely refitted again [?] for sea with from fifteen to twenty tons shingle ballast.

Capt. Wing had decided his vessel and passengers should return to the United States, to Charleston. Dr. Smith fired off a short official note that the Africans' health would then be in danger from a cold climate. Returning, however, became impossible as no merchant would advance the money for refitting the vessel. Wing wrote up a paper giving up the contract between the ship's owner and his employer, Richard Churchward, and the United States Navy, and this incompetent man fades into the mists of history, but not before he charged Mechlin $14 a night to allow everyone to stay onboard his hulk after the charter contract had failed. Mechlin could find no cheaper vessel to house the Africans, whom the Governor would not allow to be landed. Mechlin had to beg of the Governor who was perhaps the kindest in the history of Barbados, luckily:

> Actual necessity and necessity only authorizes me to act in behalf of the government of the U. States whose benevolent intentions to these unfortunate and destitute Africans have been thus far frustrated. If you will guarantee payment of any agreement I make in behalf of the US...For myself as an American and in distress I eagerly embrace this opportunity of tending my most sincere and grateful acknowledgments for the many acts of courtesy and kindness experienced from your Excellency...at all times manifested to assist me to the utmost of your power.

The Governor of Barbados, James Lyon, with his own funds, agreed to guarantee payment by the United States for a private ship to continue the voyage of the Americans.

The private ship was the *Heroine*, owned by Michael Cavan. Cavan was apparently another kind Barbadian, for Mechlin had tried to charter other ships but was quoted exorbitant prices for the voyage compared to what Cavan offered. Only three ship owners would consider the trip. One quoted close to $6,000, two others over $5,000. But Cavan told Mechlin if he could wait for his brig the *Heroine* to arrive and be discharged of her cargo then it could be had for a little over $4,000. The vessel did not arrive in port until days after she was due, but was worth the wait. She was one year old, coppered (for fast sailing), smaller but "far more convenient for the negroes owing to the greater depth of hold...affording the negroes space to stand in besides giving them as much deck room as they had in the schooner..." Mechlin explained in a letter to John Branch. "Mr. Cavan considers himself conferring an obligation [of humanity] on me in letting his vessel so very cheap."

Mechlin changed the normal food stores for the Africans to "rice and molasses...more healthy and preferred by the negroes to anything else...I have also added a few barrels of bread in case of bad weather when rice cannot be cooked" and no doubt because of the thirst suffered onboard the *Washington's Barge*, "the quantity of water I have considerably increased and taken care that it is put in new and iron bound casks."

Governor Lyon wrote to Mechlin:

> I am happy to have it in my power to bear testimony to the very assiduous care and attention shown by yourself and Dr. Smith to the comfort and welfare of the unfortunate Africans...and with every wish for the prosperous termination of your labour.

The aptly-named *Heroine*, Capt. Cole, left Barbados with the Africans aboard early in the morning of January 16th, and arrived safely in Liberia on March 4th.[163]

Chapter Fourteen

May & June, 1831
St. Augustine, Washington, Norfolk

John, the Last African

Waters Smith wrote August 25, 1830, to Secretary Branch, relating the death of one of the Africans left behind, and requesting what to do with the other. Branch in his usual manner with Smith told him to employ him to the best advantage until he recovered his health or a suitable opportunity for returning him to Africa appeared. How a sick youth could work until he got better was not addressed by Branch.

The correspondence between the two ends there. Later correspondence gives a clue as to what possibly happened next. In May of 1831 a Capt. John Ramsay of the schooner *Elvira* arrived in Washington with "a liberated African named John." John Boyle, who was then Acting Secretary of the Navy sent the captain and John to Henry Ashton, US Marshal of the District of Columbia, with instructions for Ashton to employ John to cover his expenses until he could be returned to Africa.

The same day Boyle wrote to the reverend R. R. Gurley of the Colonization Society that a liberated African had been sent to Washington "from St. Augustine." He asked if the Society would be sending any vessels to Liberia, and if so, if the African could have passage on one of them.

The reply came from the reverend James Laurie, President of the Board of Managers of the Society, who advised a vessel would sail for the colony early the following month. Boyle then advised that Marshal Ashton and the reverend Laurie communicate directly with each other as to the time and place of departure.

On June 24th Levi Woodburn of the Navy Department wrote to Gurley that there could be a passage in a vessel for Norfolk for the African and his expense for passage and for some new clothing would be paid.

By the time he left, the African named (by Americans) John had been a resident of the US for some three and a half years, from his arrival in Key West in December, 1827 from the wreck to his departure in June, 1831, apparently from Norfolk, perhaps the last African in US territory (the fate of Capt. Doane's charge unknown) who had been imprisoned in the slave ship *Guerrero*.

Four months later, on October 10, 1831, Waters Smith died. There was overwhelming sorrow in St. Augustine. Two days after his death a recommendation to the President was written and was signed by 28 citizens, which read:

> Waters Smith the Marshal of the Eastern District of Florida departed this life on the Tenth day of the present month - perhaps there has never been a Ministerial Officer of any Court, more esteemed whilst living, or more regretted when dead - He has left a numerous and helpless family, who were totally dependent on his exertions, and are now destitute without him. - Mr. Samuel Blair, is a member of this family, and the son in law of the Marshal - Mr. Blair was educated to the Bar, and for some time has been acting as Deputy to his father in law - He is a Kentuckian of a good family, and is for himself as well as for the family of the Marshal totally dependant on the Office. The death of the Marshal, and the situation of his family has excited a sympathy and compassion here seldom or never witnessed

on the death of any single individual - and we would on the force of the above fact most earnestly request of your Excellency the appointment of Mr. Blair to the vacancy - His education the respectability of his connections in Kentucky his experience in and present tenure of the office as Deputy, without other considerations would justify this application - but his connection with Mr. Smith as his son in law, as the last stay of a helpless family, as the only individual who can settle his accounts do in the humble opinion of the subscribers place his claim beyond a controversy and with hope and confidence of success we appeal to the Justice and sympathy of the President.[164]

Samuel Blair had married Waters' daughter Selina (but she possibly was his second wife's daughter by a previous marriage) four years earlier. Selina named her first born Waters in his honor. Judge Thomas Douglas of St. Augustine, who was not one of the signers of the above recommendation, wrote two letters on the same subject. Excerpts of one to Virgil Maxcy, Treasury Department, read:

It has become my painful and melancholy duty to announce to you the death of Waters Smith Esquire late Marshal of this district, Mr. Smith while living was universally respected both as a citizen and as a public officer and his death is most sincerely and generally deplored by our community...I take the liberty hereby to recommend [Samuel Blair]...to alleviate the sufferings of a worthy and interesting family and be highly gratifying to a very large portion of the people of the district, which deeply sympathizes with it in its afflictions.[165]

The second letter he wrote was to Congressional Delegate Joseph M. White, who had worked with Waters on the situation of the Africans:

> A general gloom pervades our community occasioned by the death of our highly respected and esteemed fellow citizen and marshal Waters Smith esq...As he lived universally esteemed and respected his death is most sincerely regretted by our community. He has left us, as you are aware, a large and worthy family, with, I fear, but little means for its support...Respect for the memory of Mr. Smith, sympathy for his bereaved and distressed family and a wish to alleviate their sorrows, induces me to wish the appointment of Mr. Blair...This feeling and wish is by no means peculiar to myself, but extends to a large portion of the community...I have no doubt but your feelings will be in unison with ours...Mr. Blair has no claims on you, but feel assured that the long tried friendship and support of the deceased will not, on this occasion be forgotten or disregarded.[166]

These pleas for the support of Waters Smith's family were not ignored; President Andrew Jackson nominated Samuel Blair to fill Smith's office December 7, 1831.[167]

I have not discovered where the body of Waters Smith was laid to rest. Records of the only cemetery open to Protestants in St. Augustine at the time do not show his name, nor the names of any of his family members.

Chapter Fifteen

1830 – 1843
Liberia

Records of the Africans' Lives in Liberia

So far in this book I have written little on the lives of the Africans. That is because I could not find much. But that changed when I started researching the records of Liberia, this began when I discovered that their American-given names had been recorded when they arrived there in 1830.

Some of the following records are condescending to Africans, slanted from the viewpoint of Christian North Americans, both white and black, doing the recording; but I felt it important that I include here everything I found. My purpose is to present documentation on the lives of the people who had been in the *Guerrero,* and I leave all the sociological, cultural, and religious evaluations on the Liberia situation to others.

Liberia had been settled only since 1822 - coincidentally the very same year Key West had been settled. In 6 degrees North latitude, it is a tropical country, and the temperature when they arrived in March would have been in the 90s. The forested land and Monrovia were described in a letter by an immigrant from Virginia, Mars Lucas, who arrived days before the *Heroine*, on February 17, 1830, on the brig *Liberia*:

[There] are aplenty of wile [wild] cattle and dear [deer] and goats and tame goats they are very great many of Monkers [monkeys]....

I am very much pleased with this Country. I Could not have belived, it if I has. not have seen it, myself. the soil is very rich. and very, fertile, more wood[ed] land than I thought, allthough. not much Clear'd. but. I. hope in a few years I hope. we won't have it our [honour] to say so. the natives, here is not. very. much given to Industry, or the [they] would have had more land. Cleared, the most the [they] care about is Hunting and fishing, but that in only when the [they] have no Tobacco. nor Rum. that is the Cheaf Articles the Care about, the are about the Closest people I have ever seen the would not give one mouthful if we was diing for it....Monrovia is the Cap. [capital], it is well fortified, we have 2 forts, 1 with 10 guns and 1 with 4 guns, the town is situated on a Hill, Commands a buitiful prospect, the 4 gun fort. stands about 300 feet perpendicular from the surface of the watter, 3 houses of Publick Worship, 2 methdist, 1 baptist....[168]

The settlement also consisted in 1830 of 90 houses and stores along wide streets and was 80' above sea level on Cape Mesurado,[169] which was chosen in part because it jutted into the sea, providing breezes on two sides.

There is a letter written March 20, 1830 (author unknown) describing the arrival of the *Guerrero* men:

The...recaptured Africans....were landed on the 5th, and are temporarily settled at the half-way farms; but they will, in a few days, be placed on Bushrod Island.

Bushrod Island, separated from Monrovia by the Mesurado River, had until recently been the site of Gawulun, the capital of the Dey (or Dei) tribe. The men eventually joined other recaptives, mostly rescued from the slave ship *Antelope* at a town that had been built for those people, New Georgia. It was about four miles from Monrovia.

Half a century later traveler Alfred Brockenbrough Williams briefly described Bushrod Island, at that time occupied by the Vey tribe, and New Georgia. He had hired Kroomen for a canoe trip to see the country around Monrovia:

> On this day the conscientious convictions of the Kroomen would not allow them to violate the Sabbath for less than a half a dollar per diem each, just double wages. I was forced to submit to this extortion, and off we started. Crossing the Mesurado River from Monrovia we stopped for a few minutes in "Vei Town," just on the opposite bank. This is the residence of the Vei tribe, who live there in closely built houses made of bamboo, padded with clay, and covered with heavy thatching of leaves. These houses are generally circular in form, and slope down to within five feet of the ground, where they terminate in deep eaves...The buildings are close together, with barely room between them. They generally have a little covered porch at the entrance....Then from "Vei Town" we rowed up a few yards to Stockton Creek, which here empties into the Mesurado. The creek is a branch of the St. Paul's [River], about five miles in length. The land opposite Monrovia, on which "Vei Town" stands, is Bushrod Island, forming a sort of triangle, bounded on the Monrovia side by Mesurado River, above by the creek, and on the opposite side by the St. Paul, its apex being formed by the fork where the creek flows from the river. The mouth of the latter is about six miles north of

Monrovia, (or in the direction of Sierra Leone,) where it empties into the sea over a heavy bar. Bushrod Island is therefore about six miles broad at its base by five long. I couldn't help thinking it would make splendid rice crops, as the tide rises and falls on both sides, and the water is fresh within a mile from the bar...Stockton Creek is a stream of generally uniform width, about one hundred and fifty yards, I should judge. Its flow is quiet, and its surface placid. It is one of those streams that one dreams about sometimes amid the hurly-burly, wishing that he could drift down forever on its tranquil bosom shut out by the leafy screen on each side from everything except lazily floating clouds and blue skies above. For a picture of perfect rest and repose it is beautiful. Even the brightly hued parrots and blue kingfishers that fly about among the branches and across, seem to move languidly as if infected with the general silence....By and by I noticed at one or two places on the right bank slight clearings; in which a native canoe was generally tied up. This, I was informed, was the first settlement above Monrovia. It is called New Georgia, and runs along the banks for two or three miles, the houses being built far apart. The number of inhabitants in this municipality is estimated at five hundred souls. Through the openings in the bush I caught occasional glimpses of the dark green coffee trees, or bananas surrounding some house. Then, after a while, we swept around a bend, and were on the St. Paul's, which is here about two-thirds of a mile wide.[170]

Returning to 1830, Mars Lucas described months after he arrived the want there, as Liberia was a place poorly run by whites appointed by the Colonization Society:

> Times is very Hard. out here. every thing is
> very Dear. and not to be had. The [They]
> scarcely will allow us as much provision. is a
> halfgrown Child can eat, a man can eat up all
> his meat. allin one day. We only draw 1 lb. of
> meat. per. week. 3 qurts meal 2 quarts of rice
> that is weeks allowance. I. really. think' that.
> the Socity [Colonization Society] don't,
> know, about their, Usage here...[171]

There were also fevers in the country that decimated the settlers. Half of the immigrants who arrived on the *Liberia* were dead within a year. The Africans from the *Guerrero* may have been immune to the fevers; certainly more so than those people reared in North America. In their first five years of residency only four deaths among them were recorded.

The people they joined at New Georgia also had been rescued on the Florida coast - in 1820, by US revenue cutter *Dallas*, off North Florida. The destination of the *Antelope* was probably Amelia Island, the very place the *Guerrero* people had left from for freedom.

The *Antelope* people had been sent to Liberia in 1827, the very year the *Guerrero* people were stolen from their homes and shipped across the Atlantic. The 120 *Antelope* people were sent to Liberia with 22 other recaptives[172] and named their town "New Georgia" because of their long stay (seven years) in Georgia, where they were taken to after the capture off Florida.[173]

When the *Guerrero* men arrived they were sent to Bushrod Island because, according to that anonymous letter writer,

Here they will be under our immediate notice

and control, and can be prevented from relapsing into their original savage customs, or causing disturbances between the Colony and the neighbouring tribes, both of which they are but too apt to do, when so far removed from our superintendence.[174]

Two of the neighboring tribes were described in the Baltimore paper *American and Commercial Daily Advertiser* of January 14, 1828, quoting an 1827 letter written by Liberian leader Jehudi Ashmun. Both tribes practiced domestic slavery; servitude for debts, mostly and the enslaved could be sold to Europeans.[175] Ashmun wrote

The Fey or Vey [Vei] tribe occupies the line of coast between the Gallinas river and Grand Cape Mount, comprehending a district of fifty miles, and may have extended their settlements twenty-five to thirty miles inland. The character of these people is active, warlike, proud, and, with that of all their neighbours, deceitful. The slave traffic has furnished them with their principal employment, and proved the chief source of their wealth, to the present year, when it is believed to have been broken up entirely and forever....Three-fourths of the population are domestic slaves, now engaged in a civil strife with their masters, for an extension of their privileges....Occupying the coast between Capes Mount and Montserado, fifty miles in extent, is the Dey tribe; reaching only half the distance of the Veys inland, and containing about half their population. They are indolent, pacific and inoffensive in their character: but equally treacherous, profligate and cruel, when their passions are stirred, with the Veys.

War broke out two years after the *Guerrero* men arrived, and it was over slave trading, according to the 16th annual report of the American Colonization Society:

A controversy arose between some of the chiefs of the Dey country and colonial government, that soon increased to hostilities, which proved, however, but of short duration. Several slaves, about to be sold, escaped from one of these chiefs, and sought protection among the recaptured Africans of the colony. A demand being made for them the [Colonization Society] agent requested the chief to visit the colony, and declared himself ready to do justice in the case. This chief never complied with the request, but soon after died, and his sons immediately resolved on war, and endeavored to secure the support of the Dey and Garrah kings. Several of the Dey chiefs openly united with them, while the Garrahs secretly furnished men for the contest. A few of the colonists were seized and imprisoned; one of the recaptured Africans, in attempting to escape, was severely wounded, and the town of a native chieftain (a few miles from Caldwell) strongly fortified as a place of retreat for the aggressors. A messenger, sent to the enemy by the colonial agent, was treated with contempt, and the settlements of Caldwell and Millsburg threatened with destruction. About one hundred recaptured Africans were despatched against the hostile force on the 17th of March, but, on approaching the fortified town, they met with a repulse and were compelled to retreat with the loss of one man. Prompt and energetic measures were now required. The colonial agent, therefore, on the 10th, placed himself at the head of a part of the colonial forces, amounting to 170 men, took with him a small piece of artillery, and after a fatiguing march, on the 21st arrived in front of the fortifications at the town just mentioned, at half past one at night. An attack was instantly made upon the barricade; and in less than half an hour, the colonists were in possession of the town. For twenty minutes, the firing on both sides was incessant. The loss to the colonists was one killed (Lieut. Thompson) and two wounded; that of the natives, fifteen killed and many wounded.

Kai Pa, the instigator of the war, received a wound when about to apply the match to a three-pounder, which, doubtless, prevented a much greater destruction of lives. The courage and ability exhibited by the colonial agent, as well as by the officers and men under his command, on this occasion, has left an impression on the minds of the natives, which, it is believed, will effectually deter them from any future attempts to disturb the public peace. Six of the Dey chiefs appeared at Monrovia on the 30th of the same month, and signed a treaty of perpetual amity and peace with the colony by which it is agreed that traders from the interior shall be allowed a free passage through their territories, and that all matters of difference which may arise between citizens of Liberia and the Dey people, with the evidences thereon, shall be referred for consideration and decision to the colonial agent.

The year of the war all the recaptives began to

receive a formal education. In the *African Repository and Colonial Journal* of 1832 was this:

> *Recaptured Africans* - We are pleased to learn that means have lately been placed in the hands of the Colonial Agent, by the Society of female philanthropists in Philadelphia, who at present support two female schools, in the Colony, to establish a free school at New Georgia, for recaptured Africans of the Congo, Ebo, and Persa tribes.[176]

Written in 1833, same source, quoting from the *Liberia Herald* :

> A free school for the benefit of recaptured Africans has been in successful operation for some weeks under the care of Rev. James Eden.

The men of the *Guerrero* were also falling in love, taking wives both among the native people and among the newly arrived African Americans. Perhaps too, among the *Antelope* people, who were mostly women, but, probably older than they were. In "Latest from Liberia" in the *African Repository and Colonial Journal* in 1832 is:

> Our recaptured Africans of the Ebo and Pessa tribes, were in the habit of procuring wives from the adjacent tribes: this they effected by paying a small sum to the parents of the girl; the women thus obtained were brought into the colony, clothed after our own fashion, and we compelled them to be married according to the forms of some one of the Churches, or to acknowledge themselves to be husband and wife before the Clerk of the Court of Sessions. They in a short time adopt our

habits, become civilized, and are scarcely to be distinguished from such of the recaptured Africans as have resided for some time in the U. States [at Georgia].[177]

The next year a Question-and-Answer format for a conversation with G. P. Disosway, Thomas Bell, and H. V. Garretson included this information in the *African Repository and Colonial Journal*:

> *Question*: What are your relations with the natives?
>
> *Answer*: We are under no apprehensions of difficulty with the natives. They are amicable, and bring their children among us. There have been about fifty marriages between the emigrants and recaptured Africans and the natives.[178]

The May 8, 1834 *Philadelphian* also reported the marriages of the *Guerrero* men:

> Mr. Brown, lately returned from Liberia, has informed us that a large number of the recaptured Africans settled at New Georgia, have intermarried with the female emigrants from the United States; and that in this way civilization is extending a little into the interior of the country. Their wives introduce something of domestic industry and comfort, while their husbands cultivate the earth, and are the market people who in a measure supply Monrovia.[179]

Crop cultivation had indeed become the forte of the *Guerrero* men. That same year Samson Caesar in Monrovia wrote to Henry F. Westfall in Virginia of the fine agriculture practiced by the recaptured Africans:

> I visited a town by the name of New Gorgia it is settle[d] by the recaptured Africans by the name of Ebose and Congose they had not been in the United States long enough to learn to talk English. If you could see their town and their farms...seen three crops all at one time on one peace of ground their was corn, rice...and they all look as promising as I would wish to see them...[180]

Agriculture was also mentioned in a report two years before, in the 1832 "Latest from Liberia" article. An official had visited the settlement of recaptured Africans to superintend their election of a chief. "Both the Eboes and Congoes had several times attempted" to chose a chief, the official wrote, but there had been problems with recognizing majority rule. He described New Georgia:

> These people occupy two very neat and well built villages, near the east bank of Stockton Creek, and distant from Caldwell, about three miles; a small rivulet separates that of the Eboes from the Congo village. Each tribe have built by voluntary subscription and joint labour, a house of worship, and a town or palaver house; their gardens are well enclosed, in which are successfully cultivated, beans, cabbages, melons, yams &c.; these they dispose of at the Cape in exchange for such articles as their necessities require. Adjacent to the village, but separated from it by a strong fence, are their farms, at present in a high state of cultivation. I saw one tract of about 150 acres planted in cassada, interspersed with patches of Indian corn and sweet potatoes. Their vegetables appeared to

be very thriving and will without doubt yield abundant crops. These people are decidedly the most contented and independent of any in the colony and are rapidly improving in intelligence and respectability - they not only raise sufficient for their own consumption, but have considerable surplus produce, for which they find a ready market. When not employed in the cultivation of their farms, they turn their attention to sawing lumber and making shingles. Many of the Congo tribe can read and have established a Sunday school, which is regularly attended by both children and adults; those who have received any education, officiating as teachers to the others not possessed of that advantage. These, as well as the Eboes, are very desirous that a school should be established among them.

The situation in Liberia for most of the people continued to be always poor. Jesse Lucas, Mars Lucas' brother, wrote in 1836,

I have not eaten once of flour for four years - The meat when I receive any is monkey ore something like a rat....I don't know when my Brother will marry for times are so hard he is afraid he or his lady would starve to death...There has been so much war in the country that it has made hard times for the country people...[181]

John B. Russwurm,[182] once editor of the New York paper *Freedom's Journal*, who had migrated to Liberia four months before the *Guerrero* people left Florida even considered leaving it six years later.[183]

Thomas H. Buchanan, who arrived in 1836 to

superintend the settlement of Bassa Cove, wrote that year of a second settlement by the recaptured Africans, at Capetown:

> I visited New Georgia, Capetown, and Caldwell, on Tuesday last. With all these towns I was much pleased, but this term is too feeble entirely to convey the delightful emotions excited by the appearance of things in the two first-named villages, which are the residences of the recaptured Africans. Imagine to yourself a level plain of some two or three hundred acres, laid off into square blocks, with streets intersecting each other at right angles, as smooth and clear as the best swept sidewalk in Philadelphia, and lined with well-planted hedges of cassada and plum; houses surrounded with gardens, luxuriant with fruit and vegetables; a school-house full of orderly children, neatly dressed and studiously engaged; and then say whether I was guilty of extravagance in exclaiming as I did after surveying this most lovely scene, that had the Colonization Society accomplished nothing more than had been done in the rescue from slavery and savage habits of these three hundred happy people, I should be well satisfied.[184]

In the Colonization Society's annual report of 1838 is a description of New Georgia and of a third settlement of recaptured Africans:

> New Georgia is located on Stockton creek, about four miles from Monrovia, with about 300 inhabitants, chiefly recaptured Africans, of the Ebo and Congo tribes. These people, but lately captives in slave vessels, are remarkable for good order, industry, and a

desire of improvement.   There are two
schools in the settlement....Marshall, the last
settlement planted by the American
Colonization Society, and yet an infant
establishment, is situated at the Junk river,
near its entrance into the sea.   It contains
about 150 inhabitants, chiefly recaptured
Africans.[185]

Marshall was below Cape Mesurado about 25 miles.
It was described, in 1834, as

At least three miles from any mangrove
swamps or other sources of disease, and
fanned by the uncontaminated breezes of the
ocean, that rolls its waves upon its beach. A
few houses were erected here...by Mr. Pinney.
A town of more than a mile square was laid
off in 392 lots during the last spring, and a
number of the colonists and recaptured
Africans removed thither and commenced the
construction of houses and the cultivation of
the soil.[186]

In 1839 the editor of the *Liberia Herald*, Mr. Teague,
wrote of the life he had seen at New Georgia. His host's
name there was Davis, and there were seven Africans listed
with the surname of Davis who had arrived on the *Heroine* in
1830:

Our host was anxiously awaiting our arrival,
and had made ample preparation for our
receptions. The house, a neat wooden cottage
about twenty feet by sixteen, finished in a
style that indicated a laudable ambition in the
master, displayed in its interior all the
paraphernalia that are ordinarily found in the
cottage of the decent liver in America. Of a

piece with the house was the garniture of the table. Fish, fowls, meats, rice, cassava, and potatoes, abundant and well served up, was the fare set before us at each meal, all of which was rendered doubly palatable by the cordiality and hearty welcome with which brother Davis served us. *Help yourself*, said he, *no be Mexico man; any ting you see, eat em: pese man come my house, I like see him eat plenty*: while with great difficulty we had prevailed on him to join us at table, insisting on waiting till we had finished. We had selected this instance as a fair specimen of these people's general hospitality. At Church on the Sabbath, their conduct was not only pleasing, but exemplary. There was a large number of persons from the Cape, and the church was filled to overflowing - and as soon as a stranger was seen standing for want of a seat, some one of the New Georgians would arise and tender the stranger his, until at length they were all standing in the aisle or without the door, while the strangers occupied the seats.

Liberia historian Tom W. Shick found an 1840 account of the Africans. A visitor recorded that those of New Georgia referred to themselves as "Americans" and were living comfortable lives, each family having a musket and furniture in their house, and "feel greatly superior to the natives around them."[187]

A census taken in September, 1843 at New Georgia[188] gives some details on the lives of a few of the men who were listed as arriving on the *Heroine*. By then New Georgia had 11 percent of Liberia's population: 263 people of the country's 2,388.[189]

Anthony Smith was 45 when the census was taken, making him about 29 when forced aboard the *Guerrero* in

119

1827. He was listed as a farmer who had no education and was in good health. He had married Caroline Smith, twenty years his junior. Caroline had arrived in the colony in December, 1831. They had a daughter, Margaret, who was then 6 and attending school. There were six other members of the household, two born in the colony: George Smith, 12, and Mary Smith, 10, orphans, and Cafara Smith, 30, William Smith, 26, Thomas Smith, 20, and Peter Smith, 16, who all had arrived with Anthony's wife Caroline from the United States.

James Kinsley was 31 when the New Georgia census was taken and therefore about 15 when in the *Guerrero*. From his surname there can be little doubt that he was once on the Kingsley plantation.[190] He was listed as a farmer with no education and in good health. He had two sons, Thomas Kinsley, then 6 and in school and Josiah Kinsley, then 4. He may have adopted Monday Kinsley, then 14, orphan, born in the colony c. 1829. Also in the household was Martha Hill, 18, his wife's sister. No spouse was listed so perhaps James had been widowed. But he too had married an American, for Hill arrived in the colony in June, 1837.

Sampson Lewis was 34 in 1843, and thus about 18 when considered human "cargo" of the *Guerrero*. He was listed as a farmer with no education and in good health. He had married Diana, nine years his junior, who had arrived at the colony in June, 1830. Living with them were America Lewis, 12, born in the colony, Diana's nephew, and Mary Smith, 16, and Elizabeth Smith, 17, Diana's sisters who arrived with Diana.

Henry Williams was listed as a "lounger" and in good health in 1843, when he was 35. He would have been about 19 when in the *Guerrero*. He had married Amy, then 26, who was a washerwoman. She had arrived in the colony in January, 1832. Living with them was Amy's son, Lewis Davis, age 6.

Henry Kinsley, then 42, was a farmer with no education and in good health. He was about 26 when in the *Guerrero* and subsequently enslaved, I believe, on the

Kingsley Plantation. He had married a younger woman, Louisa, then 28. She arrived at Liberia in January, 1833. Their names are followed on the list by William Kinsley, 12 and John Kinsley, 10, who were Louisa's brothers, and by the name of their son, Samuel Kinsley, then 2. Colinette Mead, 15, and orphan Louisa Davis, 12, lived with them. They had arrived with Louisa in 1833.

William Kinsley was 42 at the time of the New Georgia census and hence about 26 when in the *Guerrero*. Listed as a farmer with no education and in good health, he had married Lucy, 10 years his junior, who had arrived in March, 1833. They had a daughter, Sarah, then 7.

Horatio Bridge, a US Navy officer, also saw New Georgia in 1843 or 1844, and wrote, "We landed likewise at New Georgia, a settlement of recaptured Africans. There was here a pretty good appearance, both of people and farms."[191] Later in his journal he wrote of a man who surely was one of the *Guerrero* men. He attended a government council meeting in Monrovia, and the question of the day was on building a market-house there at government expense. This was debated:

> One of the members was a wilder specimen of humanity than even our legislative bodies at home have ever presented to an admiring world. He was a re-captured African, representing New Georgia, an uncouth figure of a man, who spoke very broken English, with great earnestness, and much to the amusement of his brother counsellors and the audience generally. I regret my inability to preserve either the matter or the manner of so original an orator.[192]

In New Georgia, Capetown, and Marshall there were men with families, homes, occupations; who were self-governing, and *free*. And none of that could have happened were it not for Lt. Holland and his truly brave Royal Navy men on a small vessel who chased a heavily-armed slaver, for equally brave Americans who rescued them from a ship heeled over on its side in rough seas and who had laid on arms all night long on the *General Geddes* to protect them from the slave traders, for the care given in Key West by William Pinkney and Deputy Marshal Fielding A. Browne, a man who would not be bribed, and the other citizens of Key West who prepared to fight for them should the slave traders arrive there, for the kind, dutiful, and persevering US Marshal Waters Smith and for A. Hamilton Mechlin, who did in Barbados what he had to do, and for a generous Governor of Barbados, James Lyon.

Thank you, gentlemen. It has been my privilege to meet you in the archives.

Mr. Teague, the editor who visited New Georgia in 1839, ended his observations with this:

> **These people were once...the victims of a cruel and relentless avarice - the doomed of slavery and bitter scorn...in a propitious hour they were rescued from a monster's fangs, their chains unrivetted, and they [were] brought back to the land of their fathers, where now they sit and worship under their own vine and fig tree, none making them afraid.**[193]

Epilogues

The wreckers' claim for salvage was regarded with little interest. On March 6, 1828, John Geddes, 51, died suddenly of a ruptured blood vessel in his brain. The same month the repaired *Nimble* sailed from Jamaica back to her station in the waters off North Cuba. Also in that month John Morrison returned to Charleston and met with Charles Edmonston, who wrote to Clay, "Permit me, sir, to beg that you will at your convenience inform me if any further progress has been made in the matter."[194]

Edmonston, living in the elegant house he built in 1825 that still stands at 21 East Battery in Charleston[195] was trying another tack for getting the wreckers paid: they should be paid a bounty for each African they had rescued from the slave ship, the same as US Navy men were. He had written to the Department of State (probably Clay) and then to Southard, whose Department of the Navy controlled the bounty funds. Southard replied to Edmonston:

> I have received your letter...respecting salvage in saving certain Africans and carrying them into Key West; there's no authority under the laws of Congress to pay in a case of this description, nor any appropriations out of which it can be paid. The power of the Executive is limited by the laws of 20th April 1818 and March 1819, which it is believed give him no authority to pay the claims now made...[196]

Lt. Holland had written Vice-Admiral Charles E. Fleming, his superior, from Jamaica on January 28, 1828. On April 16th Fleming, then aboard the 32-gun frigate *Barham* at Nassau wrote to British Minister Vaughan:

Relative to the claim made by some persons at Key West...by the enclosed statement of Lt. Holland you will observe that the delay in arranging the salvage has been entirely on the part of the salvors; for if they had claimed a fair or reasonable sum or agreed to submit the case in time to a competent tribunal the whole might long since have been arranged; and will be so whenever the determination of the salvors is made known for which purpose I intend to dispatch a vessel to Key West, the *Nimble* only having lately returned from...Jamaica.[197]

Lt. Holland returned to Key West in May, to settle the account with the wreckers. The papers of that meeting have not been discovered in the British archives. They do exist at the National Archives in Washington, but are extremely light and some words cannot be determined:

Key West
May 7, 1828

To Edward Holland, Esquire

Sir,

As you have intimated a wish to settle salvage in the case of HBM Schooner *Nimble* and without reference to an arbitration or a court of admiralty I have thought proper to confer with some of the persons who are equally interested with me in the business and after mature reflection on the subject have come to the following conclusions, that considering the value of the vessels and the amount of goods saved from the guineaman all of which

I could have saved had I been permitted to do so...$5,000 is a fair compensation. Should that sum not accord with your views I would be much pleased to have it left to a court of admiralty to decide...

John Morrison

HBM Schooner *Nimble*
Key West
May 7, 1828

500 Pound Sterling [about $2,500] appears to me a most ample and liberal compensation for the services rendered this schooner and which I now offer you.

Should you not think it proper to accept this sum will you submit your claims to be settled by arbitration by the Chamber of Commerce at Nassau...

Edward Holland

Key West
May 7, 1828

To Edward Holland, Esquire
Commander, HBM Schooner *Nimble*

Sir,

Your note of this date is received and I am ____ ___ ___that your proposition cannot be accepted. I am now obliged ____ I have ___ submit to a court of admiralty in the United States which I think is the most proper mode and the circumstances decided within its jurisdiction. I am, sir, your most respectful obedient servant,

John Morrison

There was a reply by Holland to this, but few words of it can be read. These notes were brought from Key West to Charleston (a Charleston notary certified they were true copies on May 25th) and sent on to Henry Clay by Edmonston on May 31, 1828, along with this:

It has also been stated to me in a...letter from Key West that the *Nimble* was valued at $12,000 and that...there were $9,000 worth of gold dust,[198] many packages of valuable dry goods [booty from the pirated merchant ships], a new set of sails [all salvaged by the British from the *Guerrero*]. The writer [no doubt John Morrison] of that letter therefore believes that the claim of $5,000 was quite moderate....Lt. Holland as stated in his last note to Mr. Morrison has refered the matter to the British minister and the cabinet...your continued attention to it, the effect of my earnest hope and confidence that under your auspices it will be speedily and satisfactorily adjusted.[199]

And here, at least in my research to date, ends the paperwork of the efforts of the wreckers to be paid by the British for saving HBM *Nimble* from and repairing the damaged suffered on the coral rocks of Carysfort Reef.

In London in October, 2002, I handled the actual log of HBM *Nimble*. I learned the *Nimble* had never returned to Key West, although in May she was back on station near

Orange Cay. Holland must have arranged other passage on another vessel, even though his second note is marked "HBM Schooner *Nimble*." He did not bring the *Nimble* back to Key West apparently still fearing the Key West wreckers would seize and sell for a salvage award through their village "tribunal" His Britannic Majesty's schooner *Nimble*.

Although in 1828 Secretary of the Navy Samuel Southard had refused to pay bounty for the saving of the Africans one of the wreckers, Samuel Sanderson, pursued the idea. He began filing papers in 1834, via Representative White. Nine years after the wrecking the Congressional Committee on Claims made a report which read, in part:

> The committee sees no good reason why compensation should not be made by the U.S. to Capt. Sanderson, for his services and expenses in relieving the Africans from their perilous condition on board the *Guerrero*, and delivering them to the proper officers at Key West. It was an act of humanity...in accordance with the general policy of our Government on this subject....The petitioner prays "for the same compensation as by law would have been given for recapturing the same number of slaves by any armed vessel of the United States."

The law of March 3, 1819, on the slave trade provided a $25.00 bounty to the officers and crews of warships and revenue cutters, "for each and every negro... delivered to the marshal or agent, duly appointed, to receive them, and the Secretary of the Treasury is hereby authorized and required to pay..."

The report contained also a new possible twist to the

127

ordeal on Carysfort Reef never before noted by anyone involved: that Sanderson had turned down a bribe by the Cubans to take the Africans to Cuba, a bribe of "two doubloons a head." Sanderson also related that he had supported them for seven days, the latter not true at all. (They were rescued December 20th and delivered to Pinkney at Key West on the 22nd; who put them in charge of Deputy Marshal Browne on the 23rd[200] and their expenses paid for by Waters Smith.) As to the disappearance of Austin Packer - was that because he had accepted a bribe to take the Africans to Santa Cruz?

I personally don't believe it. Lightship keeper John Whalton's begging to depart from the scene of the wrecking is certainly an indication of what everyone - especially Lt. Holland and John Morrison - thought the Cubans would, and then, did do. Bribe money wasn't needed on Carysfort Reef, for force would do just fine. But nine years later Sanderson comes up with a story for the guys in Washington.

William Wright, the Irish seaman from the *Thorn*, was questioned on the same subject in Havana by Kilbee & Macleay; whether the Americans had been bribed. Perhaps Kilbee & Macleay were being influenced by Lt. Holland, then there, who by then was surely terrifically upset with all Americans; their demanding duties, holding his rescued Africans, demanding salvage fees on the spot. Wright said that,

> He does not know whether the master of the American schooner [the *Thorn*] was induced to take the step of quitting the British schooner of war by the promises [of money] or the threats of the Spaniards, but he conceives that resistance would have been of little avail as the latter amounted to fifty two, while the American crew consisted at that time only of eight.

And as to the hijacking he testified:

> The cable was cut, as this deponent verily believes, by those Spaniards, and the schooner put to sea altho' fired upon by the aforesaid British schooner; That she was navigated by the Spaniards...[201]

The Committee on Claims reported that Sanderson's case was not precisely the same as a rescue by those in the Navy or Revenue Cutter services, but was "very strongly analogous" and suggested Sanderson be awarded the same bounty.

Sanderson received his $3,025, plus, in error, another $1,016. The error was caught in 1839 by the Treasury Department. On November 3, 1840 a judgment was entered against Samuel Sanderson in the Superior Court for the Southern District of Florida at Key West. A writ of attachment for his property was issued November 25th and returned May 3, 1841, without funds, for Sanderson had told the deputy marshal at Key West that "he was unable to pay the amounts or any part thereof." There was a notation on the returned writ that the marshal could find no property.[202] It is unbelievable that Sanderson, a wrecker for over a decade, did not so much as own a vessel. I believe Sanderson's veracity especially in regard to the bribe is questionable.

In the first half of 1830, just as John Branch's efforts regarding the *Guerrero* Africans were ending, US schooner *Grampus* captured the Spanish slaver *Feniz* coming from Africa enroute to Cuba off Hispaniola for attempted piracy on an American vessel. The Africans aboard were brought first to Key West, then to Pensacola and then to New Orleans.

On August 18, 1830 Attorney General John

MacPherson Berrien wrote to Branch that the case of those Africans was not within the provisions of the existing laws. John Branch had to immediately deal with more recaptive Africans.

In 1832 a prize list was completed for the capture of the slave ship *Guerrero*. The men of HBM *Nimble* were, four and a half years after the wrecking, rewarded by the British government for their valiant effort.[203]

Two of the wreckers, John Walker and Joseph Bethel, the latter the pilot on the *Thorn*, who once made a living from ships wrecked on the reef later became lightship and lighthouse keepers at the Keys. They made a living by tending lights to keep ships from - wrecking on the reef!

HBM *Nimble* under other captains captured other slavers off Cuba, and Lt. Holland spent much of his career seizing slavers - none yet laden with human beings - off the coast of Africa.

The log of the US Revenue Cutter *Marion* reveals that the *Nimble* was in the Florida Straits March 4, 1829: "March 2, Key West...March 3, underway...for sea, March 4 Spoke to...HBM schooner *Nimble* on a cruise. At 5 came to anchor in Havana."[204] Lt. Holland had been transfered from the schooner in 1828.

The log of HBM *Monkey*[205] shows the *Nimble* was near Bimini and assisted the *Monkey* after the *Monkey* captured the Spanish slaver *Midas* enroute to Cuba in June, 1829, already mentioned. The *Midas* left Africa two months before with 562 Africans. At the time of her capture only

369 were still alive, and 78 of those people died before the *Monkey* and *Nimble* brought the slaver into Havana.[206]

In November, 1829 the *Nimble* under Lt. Joseph Sherer captured the *Gallito* with 136 Africans aboard.[207] In 1833, under Lt. Charles Bolton, she fought a battle with the *Joaquina* off the Isle of Pines, Cuba, laden with the survivors of the 348 Africans the *Joaquina* had taken aboard at the River Bonny. The *Nimble* brought the *Joaquina* into Havana.[208]

That same year the *Nimble* brought into Havana the *Negrito* with 490 Africans on board. Those freed Africans were sent to British Trinidad due to the threat of cholera in Havana at the time.[209]

The *Nimble* had been purchased by the British Navy in 1826, a year before she chased the slave ship *Guerrero*. She was perhaps purchased because she was fast sailing; suitable for pursuit - or, in her former use, for flight, for before her purchase she was the *Bolivar*, a slave ship.[210]

HBM *Nimble* was lost on November 4, 1834, under the command of Lt. Bolton, after running ashore the schooner *Carlota* near Neuvitas, Cuba. Lt. Bolton put the 272 rescued Africans onboard his vessel, but running into bad weather the *Nimble* wrecked on a reef when the noise of the Africans aboard drowned out the sound of breakers off Cayo Verde. Seventy of the Africans perished in the sea.[211]

The remains of the floating prison *Guerrero* still lay undiscovered by divers somewhere in the tropical shallow waters off the Upper Florida Keys, while the Spanish moss in the trees at the Kingsley Plantation weeps above the remains of slave cabins.

Appendix One

Before Becoming Human Cargo

The other appendixes in this book have directly to do with the wrecking of the *Guerrero* and aftermath, the people in the hold, or of Key West. This one does not, but I thought it very important to include it, for it reveals what captive people such as those in the *Guerrero* had endured even before they were laden as human cargo.

The following was written in 1850 but refers to events of the 1830s. It is not about the vicinity where I believe the *Guerrero* people were captured, sold, and laden, but in another area of Africa, one near where some of the survivors - the 92 that arrived at Liberia - would come to live in the same decade. The author is James Hall, M.D., and he related that British warships had blockaded a slave trading depot and successfully so; that the slave traders broke up their barracoons and surrendered the captives in them. His account was published in the annual report of the Colonization Society in 1850. It is excerpted here:

> To enable those, not familiar with the slave marts on the West Coast of Africa, to estimate the importance of the annexation of Gallinas to Liberia, it is necessary to give a brief sketch of their location and extent and of the late history of Gallinas. Previous to the founding of the colonies of Liberia, the slave trade was rife throughout the whole of what is termed the Grain Coast; in fact, from the Gambia to Cape Palmas, an extent of over 1,500 miles of coast line, excepting only, Sierra Leone and its immediate dependencies.

The very heart of this extensive slave mart was Gallinas, to which only, Cape Messurado was second in importance. That the small band of colonists, which boldly located themselves on this beautiful headland...should have been able to maintain their position amidst the powerful combined influence and action of slavers' gold and savage natives will ever remain a marvel in the history of that Colony. But they did maintain, not only their existence but their integrity and fair fame, and although it required many years in its accomplishment and all of blood and treasure which they had to give, the Liberians succeeded effectually in eradicating this traffic from the limits of their territory. After the firm establishment of the colony, the slave trade on the windward coast, or to the North and West of Cape Palmas, was mainly confined to some Portuguese settlements at Bissaos, the Rio Grande, the Nuez and Pongos, Gallinas and its vicinity, Grand and Little Bassa, New Cesters and Trade Town. The Bissaos and the river factories to the windward of Sierra Leone were never very prosperous, the slavers finding it extremely difficult to escape from them without being intercepted by the British cruisers. The small factories at the Bassas were much interrupted by the colonies and finally extirpated by the purchase of Grand Bassa in 1832, while those at New Cesters and Trade Town were more or less connected with and dependent upon those at Gallinas.

The Gallinas river enters the Atlantic in latitude about 7 1/2 degrees, between Grand Cape Mount and Cape St. Ann, near one hundred miles northwest of Cape Messurado or Monrovia. The name of the river is given to the cluster of slave factories near its mouth. This place possesses no peculiar advantages for any species of commerce, and derives its importance, exclusively, from the establishment of the slave factories there. The land in the vicinity is very low and marshy, the river winds sluggishly through an alluvion of Mangrove marsh, forming innumerable small islands. The bar at its mouth is one of the most dangerous on the coast, being impassable at times in the rainy season. It is located in what is termed the Vey Country, the people of which, are distinguished for their cleanliness, intelligence, and enterprize in trade. How long Gallinas has maintained its importance as a slave mart, we are unable to say, but at the time of our first visit to Liberia in 1831, its reputation was very extended and its influences most deeply felt in the colony. It was estimated that near 10,000 slaves were, about that period annually shipped from this place alone....

We first visited Gallinas in 1837, at a time when the trade at this place was on the decline and [resident Spanish slave trader Pedro] Blanco was about leaving the coast. The first peculiarity we noticed in entering the river, was, the arrangements of watch-boxes, or look-outs, consisting of seats protected from the sun and rain, erected some fifty or one hundred feet from the ground, either on poles fixed in the earth, or on some isolated, high tree, from one of which the horizon was constantly swept by a good telescope, to give prompt notice of the approach of any vessel, and long experience rendered these men very expert in determining the character of any visitor, whether neutral, friend or foe.

About a mile from the river's mouth we found ourselves among a cluster of islands, on each of which was located the factory of some particular slave merchant. The buildings, generally, consisted of a business room, with warehouse attached, filled with merchandize and provisions, and a barracoon for the slaves; the whole built by setting rough stakes or small trees into the ground, these being wattled together with withes and covered with thatch. That, containing the slaves, being much the strongest and generally surrounded by, or connected with, a yard, in which the slaves were permitted to exercise daily. We think there were some ten or twelve of these establishments at that time, each containing from 100 to 500 slaves. We believe one contained near 1,000, which, it was expected, would be shipped daily. Each barracoon was in charge of from two to four white men, Spanish or Portuguese, and a more pitiable looking set of men we never met with. They had all suffered more, or less from the fever, were very weak, much emaciated or swollen by dropsy or diseased spleens, and none of them particularly clean. The slaves were as well taken care of as could be expected, when provisions were plenty in the country; but, in case of scarcity, they suffered severely. Many instances have occurred, wherein whole barracoons of slaves have been let loose for want of food; and it may well be supposed their owners would allow them to suffer severely before giving them up. For this reason, and because they can be stowed more closely in a vessel, children are generally preferred to adults. We recollect going into one yard where there were some 300 boys, all apparently between ten and fifteen years of age, linked together in squads of twenty or thirty. We never saw a more painfully interesting sight than the long rows of these bright-eyed little fellows, doomed to the horrors of a middle latitude passage, probably in a [space] three and a half feet between decks. Another peculiar feature of the place was, the collection of long canoes and boats, all, kept ready for the dispatch of slaves the moment an opportunity should occur. Probably 1,000 slaves could be shipped in four hours, all things favorable. In case the coast is clear of armed vessels [patrolling for slavers], and a slaver appears in the offing, her signal is at once recognized. She is signalised in return, to come in, and if she is watered and provisioned for the voyage, and [the slave] deck laid, which is usually the case, she does not even come to anchor, but stands close in to the bar, where she is met by the whole fleet of canoes and boats, the contents of which are speedily put on board; she then stands off or up the coast again, the canoes return to the barracoon for more slaves, again to meet outside the bar as before. Sometimes, however, they are not so fortunate, even when not molested by a man-of-war. The bar at the river mouth is not unfrequently dangerous, even in the dry season, and in the anxiety to ship the slaves they run great hazards, and many a boat load of poor wretches becomes food for sharks, who always follow such boats and canoes in great numbers. We have heard from Kroomen, who perform the boat-work at Gallinas, many harrowing tales of shipping slaves from that place, too painful to report, or even to recall to memory. In fact, all connected with this trade is painful and distressing to humanity, and this Gallinas, of all other places on the coast of Africa, with which we have been acquainted, has been the scene of its greatest horrors. What imagination can conceive the thousandth part of the misery that has been endured by human beings of this little cluster of bushy islands? Of the five or ten thousand, who are annually brought to this place, each and every one has to mourn a home made desolate, a family dismembered, the blood of kindred flowing. Of this number, how many sink in these wretched barracoons from distress of mind at their wretched condition, from disease and famine; how many are sacrificed in their hurried shipment by the ravenous sharks; how many sink under the most protracted agonies in that confinement between decks, the air of which is putridity itself...

But Gallinas is [now] destroyed; as a slave mart it has ceased to exist; from its marshy islets the fiat shall no more go forth to spread fire and sword throughout a peaceful land; the marauding chief has bound his last victim, the haggard, Lazarone slaver has riveted his last fetter; the shark at the bar mouth has fed on his last slave gang; and this land, heretofore detested and detestable, is henceforth to form a part of the free and independent Republic of Liberia. In the fall of Gallinas and the annexation of its territory to the Liberian Republic, we see the absolute extinction of the slave trade from Sierra Leone to the Cape Palmas. That the Liberian Government is competent to prevent its re-establishment, now, in the day of her strength and independence, fostered by powerful nations, we have a sufficient guaranty, by what she has done at Messurado, Bassa and Trade Town in time of her infancy and weakness.[212]

Appendix Two

Log of HBM *Nimble*
December 19, 1827

The log keeper (probably Lt. Holland) wrote the day's events in one long paragraph. His writing many details during the dangers of a sea fight and a grounding is quite remarkable. I have clarified the events by placing them in a time/line order as follows:

December 19, 1827

   AM Fresh winds & squally
4:00 Ditto weather
5:00 Wore
5:30 Set foresail
8:00 Strong breezes & fine
10:40 Tacked & set jib
12:00 Fresh breezes & fine. 1 Sail in sight from the
        northward

Orange Keys

   PM Fresh winds & cloudy
12:00 Observed stranger to be a suspicious looking
        brig. I set topsail, cleared for action & fired
        2 guns to bring stranger to whom we
        observed hauling up to avoid us, made more
        sail
4:00 Strong breezes & cloudy, Chase NW 1/2 N 4
        miles. Trimmed & made sail as requisite
5:00 Strong breezes and squally with a heavy swell,
        carrying a heavy press of sail & gaining on

chase. Observed her bear up

6:15 Having closed considerably fired a gun to
bring her to which was returned immediately
by her guns & musquetry. Commenced
action

6:45 Observed chase bring to the wind, fire a gun to
leeward & shew a light. Ceased firing &
hauled up after her having regular soundings
from 6 to 4 fathoms approaching Florida reef

7:30 Observed chase on shore

7:35 Grounded in stays. Observed brigs masts go
by board.[213] Furled sails. Out boat & laid
on stream [anchor] in 4 fathoms.
Commenced heaving ballast & shot
over[board]

On Shore on the
 Florida Reef

8:10 Parted stream & drove further on reef

8:30 Drifted off in 2 fathoms, let go best bower
[anchor]. Drifted again on shore and finding
tide leaving us not being _____[illegible] to
_____[ill.] of _____ [ill.] more ballast and 1
[?] carriage [?] [gun] over until 12 a clock
Fresh winds & squally

At Single Anchor

Appendix Three

Thoughts on Location of the Shipwreck

It was April, 2004, and South Florida was experiencing a very late cold front. The dive boat I was on had left from Biscayne National Park headquarters on the mainland near Homestead, south of Miami. The Upper Keys from the vantage point of that boat looked almost unsettled, like 1827, I was thinking. Then came the captain's words that we were at Black Caesar's Creek. It was where two wreckers, the *Thorn* and the *Surprize* were anchored the night of December 19, 1827.

It was much broader than I had imagined. It is just a passage between islands but it did indeed look like a Florida Keys version of a creek. That a pirate named Black Caesar had used this place to lay in wait for his victims is an oft-repeated tale that has absolutely no truth (for there is no documentation). A surveyor having fun in the 1760s had penned the name.[214]

The boat I was on had many interested and interesting people aboard. There was the film crew headed by Karuna Eberl, who had organized the trip, with a crew of young professional people in the film industry who voluntarily joined her for this project. (One, Bob Aubrey, was overheard to say on the phone that week, "This is the most important thing I've ever done.") There were members of the National Association of Black Scuba Divers from Jacksonville, Florida (hundreds of miles away) and from Miami, archaeologist Brenda Lanzendorf of Biscayne National Park, Capt. William Pinkney, first black man to sail solo around the world, and first captain of the replica Cuban coastal slaver *Amistad*, black history expert and friend Dinizulu Gene Tinnie of Miami, and others who I did not know also aboard, as the vessel made its way to the south end of Pacific Reef.

At Black Caesar's Creek I felt I was on the *Thorn* or *Surprize* December 20, 1827, sailing towards the two ships on the reef; a British warship and the slave ship *Guerrero*.

There are six references to location in the documents. They are:

1. Statement of Nathaniel Glover, mate on the *Thorn*, of January 7, 1828:

> On the morning of the 20th while laying in anchor at Caesar's Creek discovered two vessels on shore about 5 miles to the south and from 2 1/2 miles to 3 miles apart.

2. Statement of Charles Grover, captain of the *Thorn*, same date:

> On the 20th day of December, 1827, his vessel was laying at Caesar Creek, that at daylight he discovered two vessels onshore. He immediately got his vessel under way and proceeded to them...at 6:00 a.m. of the same day he came to anchor in the lee of the vessel nearest to him which proved to be a brig with both masts gone and full of water.

3. The log of the *Nimble*, December 20, 1827:

> Carysfort Light vessel SW 1/2 W. Black Sarah's Creek N. 1/2 East[215]

In going through the log of the *Nimble* for about six months before the grounding and six months after, I learned

142

that in all those months the *Nimble* had not been at the Florida coast. No wonder the accidents occurred, for the British were unfamiliar with the reef. But then, how did they know the names of Black Caesar's Creek, written phonetically in the log as "Black Sarah's Creek" and of the "Carysfort" light vessel? I surmise that this information actually came from the wreckers the morning after the grounding, the time when those place names were written in the log. Lt. Holland at one point wanted John Morrison to go to Key Tavernier, where there was a rudder, before Morrison said he could fit the *Nimble* with the *Guerrero*'s rudder.[216] That information, and place name, surely *did* come from the wreckers, for why would a British warship's crew be familiar with spare parts laying around the mangroves at a Florida Keys wreckers' station? Therefore, I do believe the place names are accurate. Others believe Holland mistook Broad Creek to the southwest for Black Caesar's Creek, but the wreckers advising the men on the *Nimble* in my scenario surely knew where they were.

4. Statement of John Whalton, captain of the lightboat *Caesar*, anchored on Bason Bank, January 7, 1828:

> On the 19th of December 1827 at 7:00 p.m. I saw the flash and heard the report of 7 or 8 guns. At daylight in the morning I discovered two vessels on shore...shortly after daylight discovered two sails running down for them. Fitted out my first cutter, beat up towards them. About 6 miles from the lightboat fell in with the sloop *Surprize* with HBM schooner in tow.

"Bason Bank" no longer shows on charts, but it did in 1838 (see the illustrations). It was opposite of and to the N.E. of Basin Hills (a place name still on charts).

5. Statement of John Morrison, captain of the *General Geddes*, same date:

> On the 20th of December, 1827, while sailing up the Florida reef about 2 p.m. discovered two vessels which he supposed to be on shore about 8 or 10 miles to the northward of the lightship...at 4:00 p.m. anchored in about a quarter of a mile of HBM Schooner *Nimble*, at which time the schooner *Thorn* passed me with a number of negroes and Spaniards on board.

6. From the protest given by John Morrison, Samuel Sanderson, Charles Grover, and John Walker, taken at Key West January 1, 1828, by notary public Richard Fitzpatrick:

> On the 20th day of December, 1827 they discovered two vessels on shore upon the Florida Reef about 10 miles to the northward of the lightboat.

The location of the Carysfort Reef lightship *Caesar* at the time is one key to finding the remains of the *Guerrero*.

In May, 1826, Key West Collector of Customs William Pinkney reported the lightship's position as 7 miles southeast of Key Largo, 3 to 4 miles N 1/2 E from the Elbow of Carysfort Reef.[217] But that information was wrong, for 7 miles off Key Largo would place the lightship in deep water well past the reef when in fact she was anchored in a basin inside the reef - at Bason Bank, according to Capt. Whalton.

An article on the locations of several lighthouses and the lightship in the *Key West Gazette* of May 4, 1831 gave very erroneous information, placing by latitude and longitude the Carysfort Reef lightship to the *west* of Key Largo.[218] But it does give this helpful information: "Light ship *Florida* is situated on Carysford's Reef *near* the site of the old one."

(The lightship *Caesar*'s structure rotted, and a new

lightship, *Florida*, not to be confused with Austin Packer's fishing smack by the same name, was anchored on Carysfort Reef in early 1831.)

In 1833 there is information on the location of that second lightship in a Savannah newspaper, *The Georgian*, August 6, copied from the *Charleston Courier*:

> We have been favored with the following additional information from Key West: The British brig *Brothers* of and for Guernsey, from Havana, was totally lost near the Light Ship on Carysford Reef on the 16th ult....Many of the old charts of the Florida Reef, yet extant, place the Light Ship <u>outside</u> the reef, which is not correct; to render her anchorage secure, she is situated in an inner basin. This error may lead many vessels into danger, but whether it was the case in this instance, or not, I am not informed.[219]

The late scholar Thomas W. Taylor, an author of a book on territorial lighthouses and lightships, also wrote of the anchorage inside the reef:

> Captains...complained...the lights were "scarcely discernible from the outer ridge of Carysfort Reef, which is four to five miles distant."[220]

Turtle Harbor would seem to be where the anchorage was, although Turtle Harbor (which was not so named in 1827) is only three miles inside the reef, not four or five. In 1839 a captain wrote that he was abreast of Basin Hill, could not discover the lights of the lightship so fired a gun, "which caused them to brighten up."[221] A half hour later, he wrote, he was abreast of the lightship. If he was sailing at, say, five miles an hour then the lightship would indeed be in Turtle Harbor.

The *Nimble* and *Guerrero* were said to be "6," "8 or 10" and "10" miles above the lightship, testified three different men. So perhaps that is not a solid clue. What may be more solid is Nathaniel Glover's account of the ships "about 5 miles to the south" of Black Caesar's Creek.

In 2001 I changed the probable location of the wreck from near Turtle Harbor, where others believed it to be, to the southernmost end of Pacific Reef. (Although the entire area was named Carysfort Reef in the 1820s parts of the reefs now have their own name.)

I marked up a chart and sent it to interested divers with the south end of Pacific Reef marked "Gail's Guess 2001." (I was imitating Dr. Eugene Lyon, who marked up a chart of the Keys in Spain and sent it to Mel Fisher with "Gene's Guess" on it, as to the location of the wreck of the 1622 Spanish treasure ship *Atocha*.)

What remains of the *Guerrero*? From a report from Key West is record of the salvage by the wreckers. (In addition the British saved much, resulting in one of the arguments with Pinkney.) This is from the Baltimore newspaper *American and Commercial Daily Advertiser*, January 17, 1828:

> About $ 10,000 worth of merchandize, saved
> from the slave brig was brought to Key West,
> and taken possession of by the collector.

(There are no other details, as the fire in Washington in 1833 destroyed Treasury Department records for the Key West Collector of Customs.)

That doesn't include the second salvage by the wreckers that I believe took place, mentioned in the *Charleston Mercury*; their heading to "Cape Florida." So the wreck was certainly well-salvaged by everyone, American and British. And it is known from Kilbee & Macleay's information why: the valuable merchandise aboard that had been pirated from merchant ships off Africa.

Despite that information, my thoughts are that there

would have been many items left on the wreck of the ship that had so many captive people aboard - items the wreckers would not have been interested in; feeding bowls, chains and shackles, possibly holding bodies of the Africans that died.

There could be other underwater finds besides the remains of the ship (which was surely burnt by the wreckers after they had completed their salvage, as was their custom, to destroy evidence of a dangerous place) that relate to this event:

1. According to the log an anchor, ballast and shot (cannon balls) were thrown overboard by the *Nimble*'s crew to lighten the *Nimble* in 24' of water but her movement in the swells broke the anchor line. HBM *Nimble* drove further onto the reef and then off, briefly, in 12' of water.[222]

2. The statement of Samuel Sanderson:

Finding that the rudder was entirely gone [from the *Nimble*] discovered there was no other method of getting her off the reef than by lightening her; commenced throwing overboard the shot and kentledge.

(Definition of kentledge from A. Ansted's *Dictionary of Sea Terms*: "A term signifying "pigs," or shaped pieces of iron, as ballast, laid fore-and-aft near the keelson or in the limbers of a vessel.")

That was near the location with 12' of water. When the *Surprize* pulled her off she then towed the *Nimble* to the westward to 18' of water.

3. The British threw overboard the firearms that the crew of the *Thorn* had saved from the slaver when the *Thorn* was anchored near the wreck.[223]

4. Two anchors were lost by the *Thorn* when the Spaniards commandeered the vessel, which was then anchored near the *Nimble* (18' of water):   a best bower anchor, due to cutting of the cable - apparently, a fiber cable and a small bower anchor with chain, which the Spaniards slipped.[224]

(Definition of "slip" from Rene de Kerchove's *International Maritime Dictionary*: To slip, "To let go suddenly. To slip the anchor cable. To detach a ship from her anchor in an emergency by letting go the chain at a shackle when there is no time to heave up the anchor. To let go entirely.")

So there it is. An anchor, shaped iron ballast, and shot in 24' water (Item 1), more shot, and ballast, near 12' of water (Item 2), Spanish firearms near the wreck of the *Guerrero* (Item 3), and two anchors, a large one and a small one with a chain attached, in 18' of water (Item 4), all probably still there, all relics of what happened in December, 1827.

Appendix Four

Key West of the 1820s: The Lion's Mouth

In 1994 I found in the National Archives a lengthy court case tried in New York in 1828. It provided an amazing, enlightening view of the Key West of the mid-1820s. A wrecker, Charles M. Johnson, had been arrested there (he resided part time in Key West and part time in New York) under a warrant charging "civil and maritime trespass." It was a charge brought by ten New York insurance companies that had insured a brig named the *Hercules* and her large cargo. The libel stated Johnson had acted "in collusion with the territorial officers of the Territory of Florida." In the court case there were many depositions on the political situation at Key West in the 1820s - the coercion of those unfortunate enough to be on ships wrecked or grounded off the Keys to do as the Key West citizens demanded. That court case, together with newspaper articles I found in Charleston and Newport - and some found by fellow historian John Viele in Savannah - painted a very clear picture of why, in 1827, Lt. Holland with haste and determination left Key West.

In the murky ownership of Key West, Juan Pablo Salas selling the island to both John Simonton and to John B. Strong, Strong too sold it twice - to John Geddes and to George Murray of St. Augustine (with a mortgage recorded in 1824) and it was Murray who made up the territorial wrecking law. He was the president of the Legislative Council, and the author of the law. It was a self-serving law which Murray did not live long enough to profit by. But others did, with abandon.

By 1825 the wreckers and their "court of arbitrators" were getting known. The *Newport* (R.I.) *Mercury* of

November 12, 1825, wrote that that year a 76% salvage award was given by the Key Westers.

> Great complaints are now made [of the Florida wreckers]...in consequence of the exorbitant salvage usually allowed them under the law of the territorial government. It is frequently the case that nothing is left after the payment of salvage for either underwriters or owners. It is the general opinion among the well informed lawyers in Florida that the law is unconstitutional and that it will be repealed at the next session of the legislative council. It has, in fact, been over-ruled by Judge Lee in the Admiralty Court of South Carolina District...[the cargo of a vessel] was sold at Key West by virtue of a decree of a notary and five jurors and over 50% allowed to the salvors...[Judge Lee wrote] "The simple question for my decision was: the territorial court at Key West was incompetent to the trial of the case. A sale under the authority of such a court cannot divert the claimants of their property. Salvage cases are peculiarly of Admiralty and Maritime jurisdiction and in no case of abandonment or derelict do the maritime courts of England and America allow over 50%.

That same year the *Hercules* of New York ran upon the reef and was pulled off by wreckers Johnson and his son, John W. Johnson, and their two crews. Then, according to testimony in Johnson's trial, Johnson told *Hercules'* Capt. Walter Seaman that he "would blow up the vessel" rather than have her proceed on her way. The wreckers brought the *Hercules* into Key West where by 10:00 p.m. the same day a "jury" was called to determine the salvage award. The award was so high the *Hercules* and all her cargo was sold in

Key West to pay it.

Three of Key West's founding fathers went to New York to testify on wrecker Johnson's behalf: John Whitehead, Fielding A. Browne and John Simonton. Browne said all these proceedings were proper. (As Waters Smith's deputy marshal, Browne had been an honest man in refusing a bribe for the Africans so it is curious why he defended the shabby reputation of the wreckers - curious as to what lines in the sand he had drawn for himself.)

Simonton said he did not see anything improper in the conduct of Johnson.

William West, steward of the *Hercules* told the court in New York that "Capt. Seaman had no friends at that place [Key West]..." and said that prior to the "court of arbitrators" proceedings notary Richard Fitzpatrick (another founding father) drew up depositions for West and second mate William Edwards but the men "refused to sign because they were not true...that it was a bad time for Capt. Seaman - five and twenty wreckers to one man." Asked why Capt. Seaman employed P. C. Greene & Co. of Key West to auction the cargo West said "because he could not do better sir - if you get your head in the lion's mouth you will employ anybody you can to help get you out."[225]

Also in 1825 Hiram Clift, fisherman, sometime wrecker, crewmember of the *Gallant* recorded in his journal written at Key West on April 4th after the *Gallant* freed a ship from the reef, "We went ashore and called a jury and got 25 per cent salvage on $42,000 dollars we having the expences which amount to $2,200."[226]

The fishermens'/wreckers' profit was $8,300, a huge amount of money for the 1820s!

This then was the atmosphere at Key West that Lt. Holland found himself in. Frequently in port in the nearby Bahamas Holland no doubt had heard stories about Key West. The January 7, 1826 *Savannah Georgian* wrote: "[There is] a summary process at Key West by which before four or five persons, all property was decided, and from 50 to 90 percent salvage taken." And in the same paper of May 4,

"In Key West it appears the questions of salvage on wrecked property are now decided by arbitration. It would appear, however, they decide the question in what way they will in this island, the sufferer [of shipwreck] is fleeced." And in the May 23rd edition:

> It has been observed that the island of Key West is considered by merchants and underwriters an object of equal terror with the late piratical establishment at Cape Antonio [Cuba]. The evils of the present mode of proceeding at the former, in regard to those vessels so unfortunate as to fall into the hands of the wreckers of Florida are represented in a forcible light in an article in a subsequent column. We know of no obligation which should induce a master of a vessel to submit a claim to arbitration where the certain result is the loss of all which the sea has spared....[the] impossibility of selecting intelligent arbitrators who are not concerned either as wrecker, clerk, merchants, etc. [and acting in collusion in the wrecking business].

The "subsequent column" refered to was a "CAUTION TO SHIP MASTERS" announcement, warning not to submit to arbitration at Key West to avoid a lengthy trial in a District Court. It listed and discussed outrageous salvage awards given on the *Adele*, *Transit*, *Virginia*, *General M'Donald*, *Gen. Lafayette*, *Mary*, and the *Hercules*.

In 1826 Representative Churchill Cambreleng (N.Y.) presented a resolution to discontinue a Port of Entry status for Key West, "the transactions at that island...notorious." Weeks after the *Nimble* left Key West the brig *George* of Kennebunk, Maine, Capt. B. Lord, New Orleans bound to Boston grounded at the Dry Tortugas. *The Charleston Mercury* of January 29, 1828, quoted this letter from Key West:

Four [fishing] smacks came to her assistance. The masters would not consent to take the brig off for any limited sum, but would get the vessel afloat and pilot her into Key West, and there abide by the decision of the Court of Arbitrators, as they are called. The captain, poor fellow, had no alternative and consented, of course. The next day she arrived in port, and the arbitrators awarded $2,800 to the fishermen for about three hours work. The cargo was partly landed this day, and sold to defray expenses. I am very much mistaken if Capt. Lord gets off (expenses included) short of $4,000. So much for the justice of Key West.

Congress annulled Florida's territorial wrecking law in 1826, but the wreckers continued their practices under it until a real court was established in late 1828.

In 1825 Charles M. Johnson, wrecker of the Florida Keys, made $25,000 for getting the *Hercules* afloat at Carysfort Reef. In 1828 the US District Court in New York ruled he had to give $22,000 of it to the insurance companies that had insured the ship. The proceedings at Key West were *not* proper. The place was: the lion's mouth.

Appendix Five

Africans & African-Americans at Key West 1821 - 1833: Events at a Little Island

American Slaver *Cosmopolite*, 1821
Escaping to the Bahamas, 1822
USS *Porpoise*'s American Capture, 1823
Enslaved from Charleston, 1823
Key West Enslaved in 1825
American Slaver *Governor Strong*, 1826
Black Population in 1827
Spanish Slaver *Feniz*, 1830
American Slaver *Enterprize*, 1831
American slaver *Venus*, 1831
Freedom Ship *Ajax*, 1833

Florida has a complicated history, having been owned by Spain from 1513 to 1763, when it was traded to the British for their release on Spain's gem of Havana, which had been captured by the British in 1762 in the Seven Years War. The year 1763 began a period of two decades of British rule which ended in 1784 when in the complicated treaties ending wars that began with the American Revolution, Spain got Florida back. But there wasn't much control of the peninsula during the "second" Spanish period, and she ceded Florida to the United States in an 1819 treaty, to become effective in 1821.

In 1764 John Gordon, of Charleston, applied to British Governor James Grant in St. Augustine for land on "Quay West." (Quay is pronounced "key.") Since he already owned a great deal of Florida land purchased from the departed Spanish which purchases were being evaluated by the government[227] Grant wrote to London to "receive your Lordship's opinion upon it...I...postponed the consideration of it."

This little tidbit of information on Key West is included here because of this fact: John Gordon was a slave trader.[228] He was in partnership with Jesse Fish[229] of St. Augustine, also a slave trader. Slave trading was then legal in British (and Spanish) law, and Key West was only 90 miles from one of the largest slave markets. If Governor Grant had not hesitated, the history of Key West could have been very, very different. Gordon claimed to want to "settle & cultivate"[230] - on an island where little could be cultivated except salt. My conjecture is that he more likely wanted a port for slavers, perhaps a more southern British place to purchase slaves, a place to compete with the marketplace at Havana to purchase enslaved people, and thereby creating a profitable brokerage for slave dealing at Charleston.

The first known group of enslaved people at Key West or within sight of it were the victims of a hurricane, a shipwreck, *and* a pirate raid. Key West at the time, 1821, was unoccupied except for the occasional fisherman or wrecker.

The brig *Cosmopolite*, Joseph A. Silliman, master, of Charleston, sailed from there on September 5, 1821, with 27 enslaved aboard bound for New Orleans. In customs records are the names of those people (in four cases also a surname), their sex, ages, height, skin shade, and who "owned" or were shipping them to New Orleans, with that person's place of residency (all were of Charleston). In some cases there seems to be who the new "owner" would be in New Orleans. [231] The *Cosmopolite* had made this run before with human cargo. Alexander Campbell was the master in a Charleston to New Orleans voyage earlier in the year, in March.[232] The invention of the cotton gin and the subsequent huge increase in cotton production in the Deep South resulted in the shipment of a vast number - over 200,000 - of enslaved people from East Coast to Gulf Coast ports.[233]

On September 14th and 15th the vessel and the people aboard endured a gale at sea and on the 15th, at night, the *Cosmopolite* was struck by a sea that put her on her side. At this the crew cut away masts, which righted her. The next morning the wind "shifted and increased to a violent gale," certainly indicative of a hurricane, although this is the first record found of the storm. That day breakers (but no land) were seen, an anchor was dropped to avoid the pending collision with the Florida Reef, but the anchor line broke. Then the captain decided to run his ship upon the reef, "the only chance then of saving the lives of all on board." The *Cosmopolite* struck the coral at 10:00 a.m. and immediately bilged, but, in the shallow reef waters, did not sink. The next day, the 17th, the crew landed "on the Salt Buch's [Bushes] Key."[234]

The location was probably at or near Sand Key, off Key West, now the site of a lighthouse. In a second description of the event is "loss of the brig *Cosmopolite*, of this port, on Key West, as before published..."[235] It seems doubtful that the wrecking was actually at Key West, but rather on the reef off Key West.

The fishing schooner *Hiram*, of Charleston,[236] also went ashore, on Sept. 13th. Arrived pirate captains Jack White and Robert Wessels and three Latin crewmembers, John Romaro, John Migues or Juan Margy, and Raymond or Ramon Crespo.[237] What had happened to their own vessel is unknown, but they purchased the *Hiram* from her owner William Lee,[238] obviously got her sailing again, and then discovered and plundered the *Cosmopolite*.

The same day of the shipwrecked party's landing on Salt Bushes Key the then-pirate schooner *Hiram* arrived, and the pirates "took out a valuable part of the cargo, and assisted in landing the slaves." Stolen from the wreck were two pianos, oil cloth, and other goods. A week went by for the marooned, surely a desperate one, then on September 24th two Bahamian wreckers found them, saved some of the rigging from the wreck and took all the people to the Bahamas.[239] From there the enslaved were put aboard the schooner *Lively* of Nassau, purchased from the Bahamians by Capt. Silliman. On October 22nd the *Lively* entered the port of New Orleans with those African-Americans who had endured so much by then.[240]

There was an epic struggle to stay alive by hundreds of black runaways and Seminole Indians in the 1818-1823 era. Escaping deep into the Florida peninsula, Spanish until 1821, were refugees from several illegal actions by American forces near Gainesville (1812), at the "Negro fort" on the Apalachicola River (1816), and at Miccosukee (1818). These peoples' exodus to the Bahamas had already begun when in 1821 Americans associated with later President Andrew Jackson started slave hunting at the blacks' and Indians' West Coast settlements. The number of people fleeing increased, and they left Florida at Biscayne Bay and Tavernier Key, both in dugout canoes and with the help of Bahamian wreckers. Most settled on Andros Island, the Bahamas, where the unique population of "Seminole Negroes" exists to this day.[241]

In 1822 during this exodus the US revenue cutter *Alabama*, sent to find a pirate in South Florida, Levi James, seized two Bahamian wreckers in Key West harbor with 15-20 fleeing blacks on board, apparently mistaking the captains as slave traders introducing Africans into the US.[242]

The next year there was this action by the US Navy, reported in the national newspaper *Niles Register* of November 15, 1823:

> The [USS] *Porpoise* was at the island [of Key West]...a small sloop, having Negroes on board, had been captured off the Moro [Castle, entrance to Havana harbor], and sent to Allentown [Key West's name, briefly].

At the time the US "West India Squadron" was based in Key West, in order to capture pirates working off the Cuban coast who were interfering with American ship traffic between the Gulf ports - primarily, New Orleans, and the ports of the East Coast.

(Some ships in the squadron had been stationed, briefly, on anti-slave-trade patrol off the coast of Africa. The *Hornet* sailed for Africa in June, 1820, and is recorded at Key West in 1823, 1825, and 1828. The *Alligator* sailed for the African coast in April, 1821, capturing four American slavers there. In 1822 she was lost on a reef off the Upper Keys after a fight with pirates on the Cuban coast. The location of her loss was afterwards named Alligator Reef. The *John Adams* was sent to Africa in July, 1821, and appears at Key West in records of 1825 and 1828. And finally the *Shark*, Lt. Commander Matthew C. Perry, was sent to Africa in August, 1821, and was at Key West in 1822 and 1823, under the same captain.[243])

It is not known whether the Navy men in 1823 captured a vessel with black pirates onboard - not too unusual - or whether they had captured a slave ship. Their orders included exactly that - the capture of slave ships owned by Americans. Participation in the slave trade to any nation was an act of piracy under American law at the time.

Other enslaved people had also been brought to Key West by 1823. In discussing the occurrence and his treatment of yellow fever at Key West that year Dr. Mordecai Morgan wrote, "Some slaves from Charleston I believe all escaped [the fever]."[244]

Another mention of enslaved people at Key West was made in the court case of wrecker Charles M. Johnson (see Appendix Four). In his testimony of the events of 1825 William West, black steward of the New York brig *Hercules* said, of Key West, "they all steal there; if you lay down a piece of food they will be sure to cut off a piece and fill their hats and shoes full; they make their slaves steal..."[245]

The next year the *Governor Strong*, transporting enslaved people from Alexandria, Virginia to New Orleans was brought into Key West after she ran aground on Sand Key on December 3rd, then was pulled off by a wrecker, with

The slaves in a state of mutiny. She was got off by the wrecking schooner *Native* and brought into Key West....the particulars of the mutiny was discovered, application was made to the [US revenue cutter] *Marion* for assistance. 1st Lt. Franklin and an armed boat's crew was sent on board. Eight of the principals were secured in irons. Order was restored and the ship proceeded on her voyage.[246]

In 2004 I went through all of the 1826-1827 incoming ships' manifests for New Orleans at the National Archives looking for the arrival of the *Governor Strong*, but without success. I wondered, was this our own *Amistad*? Had the enslaved people overthrown the ship's crew?

In 1827 the 121 Africans from the *Guerrero* were brought to the town, and lived in Key West for 75 days. The black population of Key West was then 56 which included 21 free black males, 18 free black females, and 17 enslaved, their sexes not noted.[247]

On June 4, 1830 the US warship *Grampus* captured the Spanish slaver *Feniz* shortly after the *Feniz* was preparing, by maneuvers and other threatening actions, to rob the Boston brig *Kremlin* off Hispaniola. The small *Feniz* (formerly an American pilot boat) had been at sea for 24 days from the coast of Africa. There were 82 African captives aboard. The *Feniz* was taken with a prize crew aboard under the command of Lt. J. P. Wilson to Key West, escorted by the *Grampus* as far as Sand Key Light, arriving on June 19th. It is unknown if the Africans were allowed to leave the vessel at Key West. By June 25th two Africans had died. The *Feniz* was then sailed to Pensacola, and only 77 were surviving when it arrived on July 8th, and then on to New Orleans, where there was a case held in the US District Court of the Eastern District of Louisiana, on the freedom of the 62 who had survived up to that time, Sept. 20th. A judge ruled they were free people:[248]

...The principles of justice, or the laws of humanity, both of which cry aloud against the act of forcibly reducing a free man by nature, to a state of slavery...

*US Judge Samuel H. Harper,
rendering his 1831 decision
for the freedom of the Africans of the
Spanish slave ship Feniz, brought
to Key West and then to New Orleans*[249]

On May 7, 1831 the slave ship *Enterprize* of Boston carrying enslaved people from Charleston to New Orleans came into Key West for water.[250]

The next day Key West resident Richard Fitzpatrick (there is a street in Key West named for him) brought 28-30 enslaved people in the *Venus* from Charleston.[251]

In 1833 the brig *Ajax* put into Key West - not a slave ship but the very opposite of one, carrying 150 free and freed blacks enroute from the port of New Orleans to Liberia. Many were freed slaves from Kentucky, including Alfred Francis Russell, then 15, who later became the President of Liberia. Cholera had struck onboard - 29 died.[252] How long the vessel stayed at Key West due to the illness aboard and how many, if any, of the passengers were buried at Key West is unknown.

And it can be imagined that, once in Liberia and if the language barrier was overcome, the people of the *Guerrero* may have spoken with the people of the *Ajax* on their experiences on the little island of Key West, Florida.

Appendix Six

Biographical Material

John Quincy Adams

President 1825-1829, Adams was the eldest son of another US President, John Adams, and his wife Abigail, born 1767 in Quincy, Mass. He graduated from Harvard. In 1793 President George Washington appointed him minister to Holland and he was in London as aide to John Jay in negotiations with the British on what would become known as Jay's Treaty. He met his future wife in London. He was elected to the Massachusetts Senate in 1801 and in 1803 to the US Senate. One of his appointments was as a delegate to negotiate an end to the War of 1812 with the British, after which he was, in 1815, appointed minister to Great Britain. He was, therefore, very familiar with the British when he had to deal with questions in 1828 arising from the HBM *Nimble/Guerrero* event. He was also familiar with Spain and Florida, at least on paper, and forced Spain to cede Florida to the US. He also tried to persuade Great Britain to open its West Indian ports to American ships (the *Washington's Barge*, for example, was in a British - Barbados - port illegally). He was defeated in the election of 1828 by Andrew Jackson, then served in the House of Representatives, leading there, from 1836 to 1844, a fight to lift the rule that ordered the postponement of discussion of all resolutions concerning slavery. In 1844 the rule was rescinded. He died two days after suffering a stroke on the floor of the House in 1848, at age 81.

Joseph Bethel

Bethel was pilot on the *Thorn* when it was hijacked to Cuba. Joseph Bethell Junior, a white man, native of Nassau born 1808 took the citizen's oath at Key West June 12, 1829. Another source gives Joseph Bethel as born 1810 in the Bahama Islands - there may have been two men with the same name. He may have been the same "Bethel, master of the *Friends of Key West*" that was boarded by the revenue cutter *Marion* in 1830, on a turtling voyage at the Keys. In 1835 a list of vessels employed in wrecking included "Captain J. Bethell" of the schooner *Amelia* of Key Vacas. By 1839 until Sept. 30, 1842, Joseph Bethel was the Keeper of the Garden Key, Dry Tortugas lighthouse. He had married the daughter of the Key West lighthouse keeper, Nicholosa Mabrity. In 1841 they were parents of five children. Joseph Bethel was the Keeper of Sombrero Key lighthouse 1858-1859, and Collector of Customs at Indian Key in 1860. At the time of the hijacking of the *Thorn* he was under 20 years of age.

John Branch

Branch was born in Halifax, N. C., in 1782 into the wealthy family of John and Mary Bradford Branch. At age 17 he was a commissioner for valuation of lands and dwellings and enumeration of slaves for the Third District of North Carolina. He graduated from the University of North Carolina at Chapel Hill in 1801, then studied law, and was admitted to the bar. He served in the North Carolina State Senate, was appointed Federal Judge for the Western District of Florida in 1822, and elected to the US Senate the same year. At one time he was head of the North Carolina Branch of the American Colonization Society. He was appointed Secretary of the Navy by Andrew Jackson and served from March 9, 1829 until May 12, 1831, resigned, and afterwards was elected to Congress. In about 1833 he began acquiring land near Tallahassee, eventually owning the cotton plantations of Wood Lawn, Live Oak, and Whitehead Place near there, along with many enslaved people. He broke with Andrew Jackson and became a supporter of John C. Calhoun. He was appointed territorial governor of Florida and served 1843-1845, after which a governor was elected when Florida became a state. When the Civil War loomed Branch became a secessionist. He left Florida for North Carolina after his wife died. They had raised nine children. He remarried in North Carolina, and died in Enfield, N.C., January 4, 1863, not living to see the outcome of the war.

Fielding A. Browne

Waters Smith's deputy, Browne was born about 1791 in James City County, Virginia. Enroute to take care of his brother's estate in Mexico his ship wrecked at Key West and there he stayed. He was a resident before December 29, 1826, when he signed a petition for a federal court to be established in Key West. By 1829 he owned a wharf and warehouse between Duval and Simonton Streets. In 1830 he was joined by a nephew, Joseph B. Browne, age 16, the son of his brother John Eaton Browne, also of Virginia. A sister, Susan, also came to Key West, married there, to Thomas Mann Randolph, and stayed. In 1832 he was a commissioner appointed to have a jail erected in Key West, was a member of the town council in 1835 and elected the second mayor of Key West in 1836. He also owned the first ice house, much property, and was a principal stockholder in the Lafayette Salt Company.

Henry Clay

Clay was born in Virginia in 1777 but moved to Kentucky at age 20, married into a prominent Kentucky family and owned enslaved people on his estate "Ashland." He was an attorney and was elected to the US Senate in 1806. He denounced high seas violations by the British while in office. He was House of Representatives Speaker

163

and spent 18 months in Europe working with John Quincy Adams negotiating a peace treaty for the War of 1812 in 1814. Adams appointed him Secretary of State and he served in that office 1825-1829. The American Colonization Society was formed under his auspices. Clay died in 1852 in Washington after a long political career, and was buried in Lexington, Ky.

Charles Edmonston

Edmonston was a native of the Shetland Islands. He married Mary Pratt of Charleston in 1810 and was a merchant and a wharf owner in Charleston at the time of the protest by the wreckers of Key West. In the 1819 city directory his place of business was Craft's South Wharf and his residence at 3 Laurens. On March 17, 1821 he shipped an enslaved man, Moses, age 29, to New Orleans on board the *Cosmopolite* (this coastal slaver, on another voyage to New Orleans, wrecked near Key West later that year). He built the home at 21 East Battery in 1825; it is now a museum owned by the Middleton Place Foundation.

John Geddes

Geddes was born in Charleston on December 25, 1777, son of Henry Geddes, a merchant and immigrant in 1773 from Cook's Town, Ireland, and Elizabeth Geddes. A biographer wrote that John Geddes was "a son of a store keeper and a man of the people." He was admitted to the South Carolina bar in 1797. In 1801 he purchased the Ashley Hill plantation on the Ashley River, his second plantation, adjacent to Middleton Place on the south side. He owned another on the Stono River in St. Andrews Parish. He married Harriet Chalmers in 1798 and then, Anna Chalmers, in 1805. Anna died the next year, at age 17, shortly after childbirth. Geddes became a Major General in the South Carolina Militia. He was a representative in the S. C. House of Representatives and then speaker in the S. C.

Senate. He had an office at 104 Broad St., built the residence at 56-58 Broad St. in 1798-1800 (the building was the location of the Charleston Branch of the Freedman's Bank, a national bank for blacks, 1869-1874) and lived in what is now known as the Confederate Home at 60-64 Broad St. from 1810 to 1825. He was governor of South Carolina 1818-1820. In 1822 after his purchase of Key West (he did not sell his interest in the island until 1826) his brother George Washington Geddes (1800-1834) and his brother in law, Dr. Benjamin R. Montgomery (married to Geddes' sister Ann) arrived in March to establish his claim and build temporary buildings, bringing two white carpenters and three blacks who were owned by John Geddes - Jack, Cato, and Cato a boy. Dr. Montgomery, a medical doctor and a clergyman, apparently stayed and built the first house on Key West on Lot 5, Square 3, near where the Customs House is today. On July 24, 1822 the *Betsey & Peggy*, Capt. [John?] Morrison sailed from Charleston for Key West "with Gen. Geddes and part of his family on board." Dr. Montgomery died of yellow fever in Key West the next year, 1823, and was buried in the same Charleston churchyard as Geddes was in 1828. Geddes was a director of the Union Bank at Charleston between Broad and Queen Streets. It's possible this bank loaned money to John Morrison, who was from Charleston, to buy the wrecking vessel named for Geddes, the *General Geddes*. Geddes and his son John Geddes, Jr. were "damned" by politician Edward P. Simons which led to a duel in the street in front of 60-64 Broad St. in 1823 between son John Jr., who was shot through both thighs and Simons, who was killed. John Geddes Jr. lived with his father, and died the very day Geddes did, March 4, 1828. John Geddes Jr. died of "debility" and Geddes of "apoplexy" (ruptured vessel in the brain). Just months before, October, 1827 his only daughter, Harriet, 26, died of "bilious fever." Geddes was living at the time of his death at 122 Meeting St., by the Circular Church in Charleston. This is probably where he met with the Florida Keys wreckers over their complaints of non-payment by Lt. Holland for salvage of

HBM *Nimble*. Both the church and Geddes' residence burned in 1861. He was buried in the First Scots Presbyterian Church graveyard at 53 Meeting St. I was unable to find his grave there in May, 1994, certainly because the church members saw fit to build a wing of the church over it in 1958. He was such a notable person that President Adams wrote of his death in his March 13, 1828 diary entry.

Joseph M. Hernandez

Hernandez was the son of parents from Minorca, members of a large group of people from there who settled in North Florida, · brought by Andrew Turnbull. Turnbull treated the Minorcans harshly, as if they were enslaved, so it is with great irony that Hernandez became a slave owner, repeating man's inhumanity to man. In 1816 Hernandez purchased the Mala Compra plantation located in the present-day Bing's Landing Preserve south of St. Augustine. He also purchased an adjoining plantation called Bella Vista, now Washington Oaks State Gardens. At Mala Compra were the family dwelling (at the time of this writing its remains are being analyzed by archaeologists), a cotton house, a corn house, a house for a designated (slave) "driver" and houses for the enslaved. Hernandez had been a St. Augustine City Councilman, mayor of St. Augustine, first territorial delegate to the US Congress and president of the Legislative Council of Florida. He became a brigadier general in the Florida Militia, and fought in the Second Seminole War, taking five Seminole leaders prisoner. He was honored by his superior, Major General Thomas S. Jesup, upon his discharge thusly: "I assure you of the high estimation in which I hold your services. The cordial, constant, and efficient support...I shall always remember..."[253] The Seminoles burned Mala Compra's buildings but Hernandez continued the plantation. He held hundreds in slavery - in 1853 he sold 153 people to a Louisiana planter. He died in Cuba in 1857, leaving so much debt his heirs were forced to sell much of his property.

Edward Holland

Holland was born c. 1801 in St. Lukes, London, son of ? and Mary (?) Holland. Holland left the command of the *Nimble* in mid 1828, according to the ship's log. The Bahamas *Royal Gazette* of August 18, 1829 reported that HMS *Firefly* was launched from a building yard and "is to be commanded by Lt. Holland, who was the drafter, and under whose direction she has been built." Holland commanded HMS *Dolphin* in 1838 and 1839, capturing many slavers off the coast of Africa, all of which were unladen. They were adjudged at Sierra Leone using the "equipment clause" (having on board equipment for the slave trade). They were the *Ligeiro, Victoria, Dous Amigos* (brig), *Amalia, Merced,* the *Jack Wilding,* the Portuguese *Casoalidade*, the *Intrepido* and the *Dos Amigos* (schooner). He may have married Agness Ann, who, at age 37, shows up on the 1841 Cornwall census as being with Edward, then 40, Edward in the Navy and neither in residence at the family home at Comprigny 1, Parish of Kenwyn. John Holland, then 33, is also listed in the household, but not resident, as he was in the Marines. He was likely a brother. There was also Ellen Holland, then 22, also not in residence, who may have been a sister in law. Only Mary Holland was resident in the house in 1841, along with a house servant. The 1861 Cornwall census shows at the same residence Edward Holland, head of household, white, age 60, "retired Captain Royal Navy." Also in the household were Elizabeth Holland, his sister, age 61, and Edward's sons Edward Robert Holland, then age 12, and daughter, Elizabeth, then age 11. It might be that Holland was a widower whose sister had joined him to care for the children.

Zephaniah Kingsley, Jr.

Kingsley was born in Bristol, England in 1765,

reared in Charleston, moved with his family to Nova Scotia in 1782 and returned to Charleston in 1793 at the age of 28. He settled in North Florida in 1803, long before Florida became American territory. He arrived with 100 enslaved to work his properties. While in Havana to sell his newly-arrived captives in 1806 he purchased, then impregnated, a 13-year-old Senegalese girl who had recently arrived on another slave ship. He was then 41. The girl, Anna Kingsley, became one of his several black "wives," a relationship that lasted the rest of the couple's lives together. Anna was freed by Kingsley at age 18. Kingsley had complex opinions on race and slavery and wrote - probably while the *Guerrero* Africans were laboring at his property - *A Treatise on The Patriarchal, or Co-Operative System of Society as it exists in some governments, and colonies in America, and in the United States, under The Name of Slavery, with its necessity and advantages.* It was published in 1828. In 1837 he moved his families to Haiti because of the stricter racial relations brought to Florida by American law after the 1821 transfer of Florida from Spain. Kingsley died September 13, 1843 in New York City at age 77.

James Lyon

The kind Governor-General of Barbados was possibly from Scotland. He had served in the British military where he became a major-general. He had also been knighted, and correspondence by Mechlin to him is addressed with the initials "K.C.B" - standing for Knight Commander, Order of the Bath. He had been an officer in charge of horses to the Duke of Cambridge. In 1815 he was at Antwerp, Belgium under Major General Kenneth Mackenzie in the Hanoverian contingent in charge of the infantry. He was governor-general of Barbados 1829 - 1833. A son, William Charles Lyon, born in 1825 (died Nov. 16, 1887 in New Zealand) also had a military career. In 1831 a severe hurricane struck Barbados. One of Governor Lyon's contributions to the public's welfare was to donate his salary to those in need because of the hurricane. He instructed the members of the Legislature to

> Instruct their honourable Committee, when formed, to consider in what manner the salary usually allowed to him from the treasury of the island, can be appropriated with the greatest advantage, for an indefinite period, for the relief of the maimed and houseless poor.

> This is in truth a religious and his bounden duty, and amidst the scenes of calamity and distress which hourly present themselves to his view, to believe that he can thus contribute to alleviate the sufferings and assuage the grief of the destitute and afflicted, would be a consolation to his mind; and permit Sir James Lyon in earnest sincerity to add, that no wish can be dearer to him, than the being enabled, although in a very limited degree, thus to evince his gratitude to the inhabitants of a colony who have ever manifested the utmost anxiety to promote his comfort and welfare.

Through a document leaders gave gratitude to the Lord Bishop of the Diocese and clergy for their labours after the storm, and,

> On the paternal solicitude, the splendid munificence, the unwearied attention, both to private and public exigencies, and on the numerous instances of charity and commiseration evinced and practiced by your Excellency towards individuals during the scene of confusion and terror which so universally prevailed. No language can adequately convey to your Excellency the

gratitude with which our hearts are overflowing for attentions and kindnesses so promptly and so humanely conferred.

On July 20, 1832, Governor James Lyon announced that he intended to take a temporary leave of absence "offered to him by His Majesty." Before he left for Europe he was asked to sit for a portrait, to be paid for by the "ladies of the island." It was painted by a Mr. Wilkins, and placed at Pilgrim, the Governor's residence. There must have been suspicions that Lyon would not return; and he did not. On March 28, 1833, a mail packet brought the news of the appointment of another to be governor-general of Barbados. The people of the island took up a donation, "to be restricted to a sum not exceeding four dollars, in order to allow persons of every class to show their gratitude." The funds collected were sent to Lyon, with a request that he should buy something for himself "as a lasting token of the attachment of the inhabitants."

In the Governor's praise of those who had helped in the hurricane, he declared, "In the future pages of history these acts of benevolence will be recorded."[254] Yet his own name is now an obscure one, and I am very glad, as a researcher and author, to bring this wonderfully kind man (like his American counterpart, Waters Smith) into a more prominent place in Barbados, American, and Liberian history.

John Morrison

I have discovered almost nothing on the life of John Morrison. His is a common name and appears no less than four times in the 1820 federal census of the State of South Carolina. But from the *Charleston Mercury*, Feb. 20 and 28, 1828, is a part of a letter written at Key West Feb. 12, 1828 that gives honor to the man:

Captain Morrison is here in the elegant schr.

Gen. Geddes, of Charleston. He has just shipped a new crew. The term of service of his last having expired they of course were paid off. He has his full share of all that is doing here in the wrecking business. I believe he is most generally considered as active as any on the Reef, and one of the most *humane*.

Austin Packer

Packer was from Groton, Mystic River, Ct. born circa 1800. He was master and owner of the fishing smack *Florida* from 1824 to 1828, and before that owner of the *Union* in 1823 and after that the *James Monroe*, in the codfishery trade 1828-1831, the *Energy* 1831-1836, *Dread*, 1835-1837, and *Alabama*, 1838. While connected with the *Energy* he rounded Cape Horn, tip of South America in a Nov. 7, 1831 - June, 1833 fishing voyage in company with the *Relief*, the two smallest vessels ever to do so at the time. Packer's later activities were partly or wholly in the wrecking business. In 1835 he arrived in Key West in the *Energy* from wrecking the *Hero*. He was in Key West at least a year before the wrecking of the *Guerrero*, signing a memorial there in 1826. In 1839 he was master of the sloop *Prudence Ann* of Mystic River, destined on a voyage to Key West. The 1850 census of Mystic River shows Austin Packer at age 50, occupation sailor, and in the household were Jane, age 30, Ellen, 3, and Cathcrine, 1. He died suddenly in Hudson City, N. J. April 3, 1859, at age 58.

William Pinkney

Pinkney was born in 1789, the nephew of Commodore John Rodgers who was at Key West with the anti-piracy squadron in 1823. He was Collector of Customs at Key West from 1824 to 1829 when he was removed. His wife Clara gave birth to a son, also named William, in 1829 at Key West after Pinkney had left the island. The boy was raised by the Gandolpho family. In 1841 he was a customs collector in Baltimore. He died in that city Oct. 18, 1853.

Francis James Ross

Ross was possibly from North Carolina, born about 1785, and possibly married twice. In 1828 when Waters Smith placed the ill and blind men from the *Guerrero* with him, Ross was a justice of the peace in Duval County. He was elected representative to the Territorial Council in 1829, filed suit in 1831 in US Superior Court for the District of East Florida for 800 acres of land, still pending in said court at Jacksonville in 1833. He was a politician and helped to lay out the city streets of Jacksonville and to build roads there. His children were (possibly) William B. Ross, born 1808, North Carolina, Seaborn Ross, born before 1820, and James L. Ross, born before 1810. He later owned a large plantation in Hamilton County, Florida. He died before 1850 or, according to another source, in 1861. A deposition in 1823 gives a hint of where Ross lived and cared for the Africans: "John Jones 'had peaceable possession of the plantation on McCoy's Creek (at which Capt. F. J. Ross now lives),' for 10 years."[255] A description of the McCoy's Creek area is found in the Spanish Land Grants in a claim by Isaac Hendricks for "400 acres on St. Johns River and Coy's Creek, 1 mile above Jacksonville."[256]

Richard Rush

Rush was the son of the celebrated physician, Benjamin Rush and Julia Stockton Rush, born Aug. 29, 1780. He married Catherine E. Murray and was the father of 10 children. Rush was 47 when he began to receive correspondence from Pinkney and then Waters Smith on the *Guerrero* people. He had been by that time US attorney general, US secretary of state, and long-time US minister to Great Britain, where he studied the British Royal Navy. He became the secretary of the Treasury Dept. in 1825, leaving

John Whalton

Whalton, born c. 1794, was the Carysfort Reef lightship captain who witnessed, from his post, the seafight between the *Nimble* and the *Guerrero*, attended to and then withdrew from the scene the next day in terror of what he believed could - and did - transpire. He married Feliciata Isabela Bucciani of St. Augustine on June 8, 1819 in St. Augustine. Parish records there show that he was born in Washington, to Irish parents, John Walton Sr. (somehow the spelling of the surname was changed) and Emelia Waden. Whalton became a resident of St. Augustine and became familiar with the Florida Reef during a surveying expedition in which he was employed. He applied for and received command - no doubt due to his "habits of vigilance" - of the new lightship *Caesar*, anchored on Carysfort Reef in 1826, with a crew of six. He moved his family permanently to Key West about 1825. The Whaltons bought property at 210 Whitehead St. in 1829. Their children, born in St. Augustine, were Amelia, born April 29, 1820, Joseph Charles, born Dec. 24, 1821, and Maria Marta, born July 20, 1823 (evidently Maria Marta died in childhood). On June 16, 1837, Whalton and the lightship crew went ashore to their garden on Key Largo and were attacked by Seminole Indians. Whalton was shot, stabbed, stripped naked, scalped, and his ring finger was cut off. He was buried on Indian Key. To this day his direct descendants, the Whalton family, still live on the Florida Keys, and are friends of the author.

the post in 1828, when he ran unsuccessfully for vice-president on John Quincy Adams' ticket. He was vice president of the American Colonization Society when it formed. He died July 30, 1859 in Philadelphia. His papers are archived at Princeton University.

Samuel Sanderson (also spelled Saunderson)

Sanderson continued as a wrecker captain at the Keys for years. In 1835 he was captain of the schooner *Orion* based from Key West. In 1839 he lived on Indian Key. In 1846 he was nominated as lightship captain of the *Honey* stationed near Sand Key but declined to serve.

Joseph Lee Smith

Born in New Britain, Conn., on May 28, 1776, Smith practiced law in Litchfield, Conn. 1802-1812, and became a major in the service 1812-1818, when he moved to Florida. From 1823-1827 he was a US District Court judge. (He apparently was still judge in 1828 as well, when he made a decision to free the African interpreter Lewis from custody at St. Augustine.)

Waters Smith

Smith was appointed as an alderman in April, 1821 and elected mayor of St. Augustine Nov. 4, 1821 serving to Nov., 1823 and again from Nov. 16, 1826 to Nov., 1827. He was "Warden of Trinity Church & Treasurer of Vestry," was appointed in 1823 as Marshal for East Florida.

The mortgage he gave to Zephaniah Kingsley (which Kingsley foreclosed on after Smith's death) was probably on Smith's house in St. Augustine, described as the "Wooden house fronting on Charlotte St. adjoining Maria Andrews house bordered by Charlotte [Street] on the east by Bay St. on the north by Gabriel W. Perpall." This is the area closest to the harbor immediately south of the Spanish fort. Smith married Hannah C. and, secondly, Mary. His children were:

Waters Smith Jr. His wife's name was Mary.

Selina Smith. She married Samuel Blair of Kentucky and their children were Waters Blair, Samuel Blair, John Blair. She died before 1834. There is some indication Selina may have been Waters Smith's wife's child from another marriage.

Elizabeth Smith. She lived in New York City, married Ebenezer Hazard Snowden (born June 17, 1799 in Princeton, N.Y.) at St. Augustine Nov. 10, 1826. Their children were: Samuel Hazard Snowden - later a captain in the Confederate Army, James, who became a farmer in Ohio, and five daughters, names unknown.

Israel Waters Smith. He was age 21 in 1830, therefore born circa 1819, and died childless in 1837.

Sarah Ann Smith. She possibly married a man with the surname of Allison.

Robert Smith.

Smith mortgaged property to Kingsley on July 13, 1831. He died October 10, 1831, less than three months later. His wife died in 1833.

Samuel Lewis Southard

Southard was born in New Jersey in 1787, moved to Virginia as an adult where he became a lawyer and returned to New Jersey in 1811. He was a state assemblyman, a state Supreme Court judge and a US senator. He was secretary of the Navy under Presidents Monroe and then Adams from 1823 to 1829. In 1824 he gave orders to David Porter, commanding the West India Squadron, based at times in Key West, to send one of his larger ships to West Africa

"ministering to the wants of the African Agency [at Liberia] and thence returning in the usual track of the Slave Ships." After he left the Navy he was New Jersey's attorney general, governor, and again a US senator. He died in Virginia in 1842 at age 55. His papers are archived at Princeton University and interestingly include a number of anti-slavery and Colonization Society pamphlets.

Charles R. Vaughan

Sir Charles R. Vaughan (1774-1849) was a Privy counsellor in 1825 and "Envoy Extraordinary and Minister Plenipotentiary" to the United States 1825-1830. He may have lived in Washington until 1835. His papers for the 1825-1830 period are in England at All Souls, Oxford.

John Walker

Walker was from Rhode Island. He remained in the Keys as captain of the *Capital* - of Charleston - until at least 1831. A record of April, 1829 has him in consortship again with John Morrison, of the *General Geddes*. In 1836 he was captain of the US mail schooner *Hope* and there was a notice posted at Key West by Judge William Marvin and others on May 12th that year for "thanks...[to Capt. Walker] for the seamanship he exhibited, and for the very polite attention they received on that occasion, and they confidently recommend him to the patronage of the public."[257] In May of 1847 he became captain of the lightship *Honey* off Sand Key. In 1849 he and his crew attempted to pull a ship off the nearby reef and in doing so their boat overturned. Walker swam to the grounded ship to get another boat and rescued his men. He left the position in November, 1850. He was Keeper of the Northwest Passage Light also near Key West July 20, 1855 to April 15, 1858, and again February 1, 1859 to before 1863. A son, James T. Walker, was Assistant Keeper at Northwest Passage Light 1856-1860. He was also born in Rhode Island, in 1838.

Appendix Seven

Discussion on Identity of the Africans

Earlier I quoted a source on taking captives in the Nigeria area and another of the active slave trading there, with some thoughts that those captives could have been the people who came to be on the *Guerrero*. This is a discussion on how I have reached that tentative conclusion.

First, the populace already at New Georgia before the *Guerrero* men arrived must be discussed. This is their story:

The human cargo of the *Antelope*, too, had been pirated. The slaver *Columbia* left Baltimore with an American captain and mostly American crew under the flag of Venezuela and pirated 25 Africans off the coast of Africa from the American slaver *Exchange* and others from Portuguese and Spanish slave ships, one of them the *Antelope*, which she attacked near the Congo River. The *Columbia* changed her name during this voyage, to the *Arraganta*, and then to the *General Ramirez*. She wrecked off Brazil and the African survivors were shifted to the *Antelope*, kept in company by the slavers, and that ship then sailed for Florida.

Other recaptives had arrived even before the *Antelope* group, but apparently had dispersed. Instructions from the US to Dr. John W. Peaco at Liberia in 1825 were: "should any of them discover their nation and country, and desire to return to their homes, you will not oppose their wishes, but facilitate and promote them." There were no recaptives in Liberia when the *Antelope* group arrived.[258]

Because of the attack of the *Antelope* at the Congo River it can be fairly assumed that that area is the origin of some of the people on the *Antelope*.

The Congo people are identified by scholar Philip D.

Curtin as any Bantu-speaking people from western Central Africa, and the Eboe people, Curtin writes, would have been people shipped from New Calabar on the coast of present-day Nigeria.[259] Igbo has been misspelled as "Heebo," "Ebe," "Ebo" and "Ibo."[260] For practical purposes here, the Igbo will be referred to as Eboe, the spelling used in the documents.

References to Origin

1. There was the establishment of "a free school at New Georgia, for recaptured Africans of the **Congo**, **Ebo**, and **Persa** tribes (see page 113).

2. "Our recaptured Africans of the **Ebo** and **Pessa** tribes, were in the habit of procuring wives from the adjacent tribes." (page 113) We know that all the *Guerrero* people in Liberia were men, and that most of the *Antelope* people were women.[261] This reference, then, seems to indicate they were Ebo and Pessa (or Persa).

3. "I visited a town by the name of New Gorgia it is settled[d] by the recaptured Africans by the name of **Ebose** and **Congose** they had not been in the United States long enough to learn English." (page 115) This quote complicates matters, and surely refers to the *Guerrero* people, as the *Antelope* people knew some English from the seven years in the US.

4. "Both the **Eboes** and **Congoes** had several times" attempted to choose a chief. This writing continues to describe people living together but separately, a small rivulet separating "that of the **Eboes** from the **Congo** village." (page 115)

5. "Many of the **Congo** tribe can read and have established a Sunday school, which is regularly attended by both children

and adults." (page 116) This was written in 1832, and if the *Guerrero* men had children they would have been only infants. This places the *Antelope* people as the Congo tribe.

6. "New Georgia...with about 300 inhabitants, chiefly recaptured Africans, of the **Ebo** and **Congo** tribes." (page 117)

So there is uncertainty, but it seems that most of the *Antelope* people already at New Georgia were Congo, and most of the *Guerrero* people were Igbo (spelled Eboe). But the fact that both had been subjects of pirates means we will never know.

Appendix Eight

Chronological List of Documents

This list is of documents and items I have found in my research on all aspects of the story of the wrecking of the *Guerrero* and aftermath. Most are in the Public Record Office in London and the National Archives in Washington, but others were discovered elsewhere. All have been collected and transcribed at my own very considerable time and expense. Transcriptions of many of the most important documents - my collection through 1992 - were donated in 1993 to the Monroe County Public Libraries at Key West, Florida and Islamorada, Upper Florida Keys, Florida, to the P. K. Yonge Library of Florida History in Gainesville, to the St. Augustine Historical Society Library, St. Augustine, Florida, to The Black Archives, History and Research Foundation of South Florida, Inc., Miami, and to the Research Center, Historical Museum of Southern Florida, Miami, under the cover, "1827 Drama: Slave Ship Wrecks on Carysfort Reef."

1827

July 31	British Commissioners Henry T. Kilbee and W. S. Macleay to George Canning, Secretary of the Foreign Office, in London, written from Havana
Dec. 12	*Royal Gazette* (Bahamas)
Dec. 13	Log of HBM *Nimble*, December 13 to February 11, 1828, and notes I made in London on several months of the log before and after those dates
Dec. 23	US Collector of Customs William Pinkney to US Secretary of the Treasury Richard Rush in Washington, written from Key West
Dec. 25	Lt. and Commander of HBM *Nimble*, Edward Holland, to Pinkney, Key West
Dec. 25	Pinkney to Holland, Key West
Dec. 25	Bunce and Disney, merchants, to Holland, Key West
Dec. 26	Holland to the Principal Magistrate at Key West, Key West
Dec. 26	Holland to Pinkney, Key West
Dec. 26	Holland to Bunce & Disney, Key West
Dec. 26	Protest, the wrecker *Thorn* against the *Guerrero*, Key West
Dec. 26	Unnamed correspondent in Key West to *American and Commercial Daily Advertiser* (Baltimore), printed January 18, 1828
Dec. 27	John Morrison, captain of the *General Geddes* to Holland, Key West
Dec. 27	Holland to Morrison, Key West
Dec. 27	Holland to ? (probably George E. Tingle, Justice of the Peace), Key West
Dec. 27	Holland to Bunce & Disney, Key West

Dec. 28	Bunce & Disney to Holland, Key West
Dec. 28	Bunce & Disney to Holland, Key West
Dec. 31 (?)	List of slave ships landing cargoes in the neighborhood of Havana during the year 1827, Havana
Dec. 31	Holland to Kilbee & Macleay, Havana
Dec. 31	Deposition of crewman William Wright of the *Thorn*, Havana
Dec. 31	Kilbee and Macleay to Captain General Francisco Dionisio Vives, Havana
Dec. 31	Prize List made by Holland in Havana
Dec. 31	List of *Guerrero* Crew (Partial), made by Holland in Havana

1828

Jan. 1	Holland to British Minister in Washington Charles R. Vaughan, written from Havana
Jan. 1	Wrecker captains' memorial taken by Richard Fitzpatrick, Key West
Jan. 2	Vives to Kilbee and Macleay, Havana
Jan. 3	Kilbee & Macleay to the Earl of Dudley (John William Ward), the Secretary of State for Foreign Affairs, written in Havana
Jan. 5	*Royal Gazette*
Jan. 5	Captains Morrison, Sanderson, Grover & Walker to US Secretary of State Henry Clay in Washington, written from Key West (cover letter for the Jan. 1 memorials)
Jan. 7	Depositions taken by George E. Tingle at Key West: John Morrison, master of the schooner *General Geddes* Samuel Sanderson, master of the sloop *Surprize*

the post in 1828, when he ran unsuccessfully for vice-president on John Quincy Adams' ticket. He was vice president of the American Colonization Society when it formed. He died July 30, 1859 in Philadelphia. His papers are archived at Princeton University.

Samuel Sanderson (also spelled Saunderson)

Sanderson continued as a wrecker captain at the Keys for years. In 1835 he was captain of the schooner *Orion* based from Key West. In 1839 he lived on Indian Key. In 1846 he was nominated as lightship captain of the *Honey* stationed near Sand Key but declined to serve.

Joseph Lee Smith

Born in New Britain, Conn., on May 28, 1776, Smith practiced law in Litchfield, Conn. 1802-1812, and became a major in the service 1812-1818, when he moved to Florida. From 1823-1827 he was a US District Court judge. (He apparently was still judge in 1828 as well, when he made a decision to free the African interpreter Lewis from custody at St. Augustine.)

Waters Smith

Smith was appointed as an alderman in April, 1821 and elected mayor of St. Augustine Nov. 4, 1821 serving to Nov., 1823 and again from Nov. 16, 1826 to Nov., 1827. He was "Warden of Trinity Church & Treasurer of Vestry," was appointed in 1823 as Marshal for East Florida.

The mortgage he gave to Zephaniah Kingsley (which Kingsley foreclosed on after Smith's death) was probably on Smith's house in St. Augustine, described as the "Wooden house fronting on Charlotte St. adjoining Maria Andrews house bordered by Charlotte [Street] on the east by Bay St. on the north by Gabriel W. Perpall." This is the area closest to the harbor immediately south of the Spanish fort. Smith married Hannah C. and, secondly, Mary. His children were:

Waters Smith Jr. His wife's name was Mary.

Selina Smith. She married Samuel Blair of Kentucky and their children were Waters Blair, Samuel Blair, John Blair. She died before 1834. There is some indication Selina may have been Waters Smith's wife's child from another marriage.

Elizabeth Smith. She lived in New York City, married Ebenezer Hazard Snowden (born June 17, 1799 in Princeton, N.Y.) at St. Augustine Nov. 10, 1826. Their children were: Samuel Hazard Snowden - later a captain in the Confederate Army, James, who became a farmer in Ohio, and five daughters, names unknown.

Israel Waters Smith. He was age 21 in 1830, therefore born circa 1819, and died childless in 1837.

Sarah Ann Smith. She possibly married a man with the surname of Allison.

Robert Smith.

Smith mortgaged property to Kingsley on July 13, 1831. He died October 10, 1831, less than three months later. His wife died in 1833.

Samuel Lewis Southard

Southard was born in New Jersey in 1787, moved to Virginia as an adult where he became a lawyer and returned to New Jersey in 1811. He was a state assemblyman, a state Supreme Court judge and a US senator. He was secretary of the Navy under Presidents Monroe and then Adams from 1823 to 1829. In 1824 he gave orders to David Porter, commanding the West India Squadron, based at times in Key West, to send one of his larger ships to West Africa "ministering to the wants of the African Agency [at Liberia] and thence returning in the usual track of the Slave Ships." After he left the Navy he was New Jersey's attorney general, governor, and again a US senator. He died in Virginia in 1842 at age 55. His papers are archived at Princeton University and interestingly include a number of anti-slavery and Colonization Society pamphlets.

Charles R. Vaughan

Sir Charles R. Vaughan (1774-1849) was a Privy counsellor in 1825 and "Envoy Extraordinary and Minister Plenipotentiary" to the United States 1825-1830. He may have lived in Washington until 1835. His papers for the 1825-1830 period are in England at All Souls, Oxford.

John Walker

Walker was from Rhode Island. He remained in the Keys as captain of the *Capital* - of Charleston - until at least 1831. A record of April, 1829 has him in consortship again with John Morrison, of the *General Geddes*. In 1836 he was captain of the US mail schooner *Hope* and there was a notice posted at Key West by Judge William Marvin and others on May 12th that year for "thanks...[to Capt. Walker] for the seamanship he exhibited, and for the very polite attention they received on that occasion, and they confidently recommend him to the patronage of the public."[257] In May of 1847 he became captain of the lightship *Honey* off Sand Key. In 1849 he and his crew attempted to pull a ship off the nearby reef and in doing so their boat overturned. Walker swam to the grounded ship to get another boat and rescued his men. He left the position in November, 1850. He was Keeper of the Northwest Passage Light also near Key West July 20, 1855 to April 15, 1858, and again February 1, 1859 to before 1863. A son, James T. Walker, was Assistant Keeper at Northwest Passage Light 1856-1860. He was also born in Rhode Island, in 1838.

John Whalton

Whalton, born c. 1794, was the Carysfort Reef lightship captain who witnessed, from his post, the seafight between the *Nimble* and the *Guerrero*, attended to and then withdrew from the scene the next day in terror of what he believed could - and did - transpire. He married Feliciata Isabela Bucciani of St. Augustine on June 8, 1819 in St. Augustine. Parish records there show that he was born in Washington, to Irish parents, John Walton Sr. (somehow the spelling of the surname was changed) and Emelia Waden. Whalton became a resident of St. Augustine and became familiar with the Florida Reef during a surveying expedition in which he was employed. He applied for and received command - no doubt due to his "habits of vigilance" - of the new lightship *Caesar*, anchored on Carysfort Reef in 1826, with a crew of six. He moved his family permanently to Key West about 1825. The Whaltons bought property at 210 Whitehead St. in 1829. Their children, born in St. Augustine, were Amelia, born April 29, 1820, Joseph Charles, born Dec. 24, 1821, and Maria Marta, born July 20, 1823 (evidently Maria Marta died in childhood). On June 16, 1837, Whalton and the lightship crew went ashore to their garden on Key Largo and were attacked by Seminole Indians. Whalton was shot, stabbed, stripped naked, scalped, and his ring finger was cut off. He was buried on Indian Key. To this day his direct descendants, the Whalton family, still live on the Florida Keys, and are friends of the author.

Appendix Seven

Discussion on Identity of the Africans

Earlier I quoted a source on taking captives in the Nigeria area and another of the active slave trading there, with some thoughts that those captives could have been the people who came to be on the *Guerrero*. This is a discussion on how I have reached that tentative conclusion.

First, the populace already at New Georgia before the *Guerrero* men arrived must be discussed. This is their story:

The human cargo of the *Antelope*, too, had been pirated. The slaver *Columbia* left Baltimore with an American captain and mostly American crew under the flag of Venezuela and pirated 25 Africans off the coast of Africa from the American slaver *Exchange* and others from Portuguese and Spanish slave ships, one of them the *Antelope*, which she attacked near the Congo River. The *Columbia* changed her name during this voyage, to the *Arraganta*, and then to the *General Ramirez*. She wrecked off Brazil and the African survivors were shifted to the *Antelope*, kept in company by the slavers, and that ship then sailed for Florida.

Other recaptives had arrived even before the *Antelope* group, but apparently had dispersed. Instructions from the US to Dr. John W. Peaco at Liberia in 1825 were: "should any of them discover their nation and country, and desire to return to their homes, you will not oppose their wishes, but facilitate and promote them." There were no recaptives in Liberia when the *Antelope* group arrived.[258]

Because of the attack of the *Antelope* at the Congo River it can be fairly assumed that that area is the origin of some of the people on the *Antelope*.

The Congo people are identified by scholar Philip D.

Curtin as any Bantu-speaking people from western Central Africa, and the Eboe people, Curtin writes, would have been people shipped from New Calabar on the coast of present-day Nigeria.[259] Igbo has been misspelled as "Heebo," "Ebe," "Ebo" and "Ibo."[260] For practical purposes here, the Igbo will be referred to as Eboe, the spelling used in the documents.

References to Origin

1. There was the establishment of "a free school at New Georgia, for recaptured Africans of the **Congo**, **Ebo**, and **Persa** tribes (see page 113).

2. "Our recaptured Africans of the **Ebo** and **Pessa** tribes, were in the habit of procuring wives from the adjacent tribes." (page 113) We know that all the *Guerrero* people in Liberia were men, and that most of the *Antelope* people were women.[261] This reference, then, seems to indicate they were Ebo and Pessa (or Persa).

3. "I visited a town by the name of New Gorgia it is settled[d] by the recaptured Africans by the name of **Ebose** and **Congose** they had not been in the United States long enough to learn English." (page 115) This quote complicates matters, and surely refers to the *Guerrero* people, as the *Antelope* people knew some English from the seven years in the US.

4. "Both the **Eboes** and **Congoes** had several times" attempted to choose a chief. This writing continues to describe people living together but separately, a small rivulet separating "that of the **Eboes** from the **Congo** village." (page 115)

5. "Many of the **Congo** tribe can read and have established a Sunday school, which is regularly attended by both children

and adults." (page 116) This was written in 1832, and if the *Guerrero* men had children they would have been only infants. This places the *Antelope* people as the Congo tribe.

6. "New Georgia...with about 300 inhabitants, chiefly recaptured Africans, of the **Ebo** and **Congo** tribes." (page 117)

So there is uncertainty, but it seems that most of the *Antelope* people already at New Georgia were Congo, and most of the *Guerrero* people were Igbo (spelled Eboe). But the fact that both had been subjects of pirates means we will never know.

Appendix Eight

Chronological List of Documents

This list is of documents and items I have found in my research on all aspects of the story of the wrecking of the *Guerrero* and aftermath. Most are in the Public Record Office in London and the National Archives in Washington, but others were discovered elsewhere. All have been collected and transcribed at my own very considerable time and expense. Transcriptions of many of the most important documents - my collection through 1992 - were donated in 1993 to the Monroe County Public Libraries at Key West, Florida and Islamorada, Upper Florida Keys, Florida, to the P. K. Yonge Library of Florida History in Gainesville, to the St. Augustine Historical Society Library, St. Augustine, Florida, to The Black Archives, History and Research Foundation of South Florida, Inc., Miami, and to the Research Center, Historical Museum of Southern Florida, Miami, under the cover, "1827 Drama: Slave Ship Wrecks on Carysfort Reef."

1827

July 31	British Commissioners Henry T. Kilbee and W. S. Macleay to George Canning, Secretary of the Foreign Office, in London, written from Havana
Dec. 12	*Royal Gazette* (Bahamas)
Dec. 13	Log of HBM *Nimble*, December 13 to February 11, 1828, and notes I made in London on several months of the log before and after those dates
Dec. 23	US Collector of Customs William Pinkney to US Secretary of the Treasury Richard Rush in Washington, written from Key West
Dec. 25	Lt. and Commander of HBM *Nimble*, Edward Holland, to Pinkney, Key West
Dec. 25	Pinkney to Holland, Key West
Dec. 25	Bunce and Disney, merchants, to Holland, Key West
Dec. 26	Holland to the Principal Magistrate at Key West, Key West
Dec. 26	Holland to Pinkney, Key West
Dec. 26	Holland to Bunce & Disney, Key West
Dec. 26	Protest, the wrecker *Thorn* against the *Guerrero*, Key West
Dec. 26	Unnamed correspondent in Key West to *American and Commercial Daily Advertiser* (Baltimore), printed January 18, 1828
Dec. 27	John Morrison, captain of the *General Geddes* to Holland, Key West
Dec. 27	Holland to Morrison, Key West
Dec. 27	Holland to ? (probably George E. Tingle, Justice of the Peace), Key West
Dec. 27	Holland to Bunce & Disney, Key West

Dec. 28	Bunce & Disney to Holland, Key West
Dec. 28	Bunce & Disney to Holland, Key West
Dec. 31 (?)	List of slave ships landing cargoes in the neighborhood of Havana during the year 1827, Havana
Dec. 31	Holland to Kilbee & Macleay, Havana
Dec. 31	Deposition of crewman William Wright of the *Thorn*, Havana
Dec. 31	Kilbee and Macleay to Captain General Francisco Dionisio Vives, Havana
Dec. 31	Prize List made by Holland in Havana
Dec. 31	List of *Guerrero* Crew (Partial), made by Holland in Havana

1828

Jan. 1	Holland to British Minister in Washington Charles R. Vaughan, written from Havana
Jan. 1	Wrecker captains' memorial taken by Richard Fitzpatrick, Key West
Jan. 2	Vives to Kilbee and Macleay, Havana
Jan. 3	Kilbee & Macleay to the Earl of Dudley (John William Ward), the Secretary of State for Foreign Affairs, written in Havana
Jan. 5	*Royal Gazette*
Jan. 5	Captains Morrison, Sanderson, Grover & Walker to US Secretary of State Henry Clay in Washington, written from Key West (cover letter for the Jan. 1 memorials)
Jan. 7	Depositions taken by George E. Tingle at Key West: John Morrison, master of the schooner *General Geddes* Samuel Sanderson, master of the sloop *Surprize*

Charles Grover, master of the
schooner *Thorn*
Nathaniel Glover, mate of the *Thorn*
John Walker, master of the sloop
Capital
John Whalton, captain of the lightship
Caesar
Daniel Fitch, master of the schooner
Reuben Ross
William Bunce, of the firm Bunce &
Disney (owners of the *Thorn*)
F. [Fielding] A. Browne, Key West
resident
R. [Robert] B. Stanard, Key West
resident

Jan. 14	*American and Commercial Daily Advertiser*
Jan. 16	*Charleston Mercury*
Jan. 17	Correspondent of Key West to *American and Commercial Daily Advertiser*
Jan. 21	*Savannah Georgian* (quoting the *Charleston Courier*)
Jan. 22	Vaughan in Washington to Clay in Washington
Jan. 25	Agents for the wreckers, Charles Edmonston and John Geddes in Charleston to Clay in Washington
Jan. 27	Vaughan to Holland
Jan. 28	Holland in Port Royal, Jamaica, to British Vice-Admiral of the White, Charles E. Fleming
Feb. 7	Rush to Pinkney
Feb. 7	Diary of John Quincy Adams, Washington
Feb. 8	*Pensacola Gazette*
Feb. 8	Marshal of the Eastern District of Florida, Waters Smith, to Rush, from St. Augustine
Feb. 15	*Pensacola Gazette*
Feb. 18	Clay to Vaughan, Washington

Feb. 18	Clay to Vaughan, Washington
Feb. 21	Vaughan to Clay, Washington
Feb. 21	Vaughan to Clay, Washington
Feb. 23	Vaughan to Fleming
Mar. 4	Vaughan to the Earl of Dudley
Mar. 4	Vaughan to the Earl of Dudley
Mar. 7	Manifest of the cargo on board the *General Geddes* (a)
Mar. 7	Pinkney statement, Key West
Mar. 11	Secretary of the Navy Samuel L. Southard to the Speaker of the House of Representatives
Mar. 11	Deposition of John Morrison given to Thomas F. Cornell, Deputy Collector of Customs for the District of St. Augustine at St. Augustine, Florida (a)
Mar. 11	Deposition of Waters Smith given to Cornell (a)
Mar. 11	Cornell to Thomas Douglas, US District Attorney for East Florida (a)
Mar. 15	Cornell to Rush (a)
Mar. 18	Contract between Waters Smith and Joseph M. Hernandez, St. John's County, Florida
Mar. 31	Edmonston to Clay
Apr. 2	Smith to Rush
Apr. 2	Smith to Florida Delegate Joseph M. White
Apr. 11	Diary of John Quincy Adams
Apr. 14	Southard to Dr. George P. Todsen
Apr. 15	Diary of John Quincy Adams
Apr. 16	Fleming in Nassau to Vaughan
Apr. 18	Edmonston to Clay
Apr. 30	Diary of John Quincy Adams
Apr. 30	President Adams' Message to Congress
May 7	Morrison/Holland notes, Key West
May 12	Vaughan to the Earl of Dudley
May 21	Southard to Edmonston
May 25	Notarial copies of Morris/Holland notes by R. Herot, Charleston

May 31	Edmonston to Clay
July 16	Waters Smith to Southard
Aug. 7	Southard to Waters Smith
Oct. 27	Waters Smith to Southard
Oct. 28	Diary of John Quincy Adams
Oct. 29	Diary of John Quincy Adams
Oct. 31	Diary of John Quincy Adams
Nov. 1	Waters Smith in Washington to Southard
Nov. 5	Diary of John Quincy Adams
Nov. 18	Southard to Waters Smith
Nov. 20	Southard to John Hanson (of the Colonization Society?) in Philadelphia
Nov. 27	Secretary of the Navy (Southard) Report to Congress

1829

Jan. 13	Congressional Resolution made by Representative Clement Dorsey (Md.)
Jan. 24	Southard to Dr. Richard Randall, Principal Agent of the US in Cape Mesurado (Liberia)
Feb. 3	Southard to Thomas Finley, US Marshal in Baltimore
Feb. 9	Copy of "Case of the *Guerrero*" to Mr. Bosanquet (cover page), London
Apr. 22	Waters Smith to John Branch, Secretary of the Navy
May 8	Branch to Waters Smith
June 5	Branch to Isaac Phillips, Navy Agent in Baltimore
June 5	Branch to Miles King, Navy Agent in Norfolk
June 15	Branch to King
June 15	Branch to Smith
June 15	Branch to R. R. Gurley, Agent, Colonization Society, in Washington

June 15	Branch to Phillips
June 15	Branch to Randall
June 27	Branch to King
June 27	Branch to A. Hamilton Mechlin, Colonization Society, in Washington
June 27	Branch to Dr. John Vaughn Smith in Washington
June 27	Branch to Waters Smith
June 27	Branch to Finley
July 1	Branch to Waters Smith then in Washington
July 2	Branch to King
July 2	Branch to Dr. John Vaughn Smith in Baltimore
July 9	Richard H. Bradford, Acting Secretary of the Navy to C. C. Harper in Baltimore
July 9	Bradford to Finley
July 9	Bradford to A. Hamilton Mechlin
July 30	Branch to Phillips
Aug. 3	Branch to Richard D. Harris, US Navy Agent in Washington
Aug. 4	Branch to Gurley
Aug. 11	Branch to Commander James Barron, Navy Yard, Norfolk
Aug. 11	Branch to Dr. Joseph Mechlin, Assistant, Agency for the Reception of Liberated Africans, Cape Mesurado
Aug. 12	Branch to Richard Churchward in New York
Aug. 12	Branch to William Ropes in Boston
Aug. 12	Branch to Phillips
Aug. 13	Branch to Harris in Boston
Aug. 14	Branch to J. H. McCulloh Jr., Collector, Baltimore
Aug. 18	Finley to Branch
Aug. 21	Waters Smith at Fernandina, Amelia Island, Florida, to Branch
Aug. 22	Christian Andrews, Navy Dept. to Finley
Aug. 28	Waters Smith at Fernandina to John Branch
Aug. 29	*The Niles Register*

Sept. 19	Branch to Barron
Sept. 21	Declaration of President Andrew Jackson, Washington
Sept. 22	Secretary of the Navy to President Andrew Jackson
Sept. 23	Branch to Dr. Joseph Mechlin in Liberia
Sept. 23	Branch to Phillips
Sept. 29	*Florida Herald* (St. Augustine)
Sept. 30	*Florida Herald*
Oct. 2	Branch to Phillips
Oct. 7	Branch to A. Hamilton Mechlin at Fernandina
Oct. 7	Branch to Waters Smith at Fernandina
Oct. 7	Branch to Churchward, then at Norfolk
Oct. 28	Branch to Churchward
Oct. 29	Branch to Amos Kendall, Fourth Auditor of the Treasury
Oct. 30	Branch to Waters Smith
Nov. 2	Waters Smith vs. Joseph M. Hernandez, St. John's County, Florida
Nov. 11	Christian Andrews to Kendall
Dec. 31	A. H. Mechlin aboard the *Washington's Barge* to His Excellency Governor of Barbados James Lyon
Dec. 31	Capt. A. H. Wing in Barbados to A. H. Mechlin in Barbados
Dec. 31	Statement by ship builders and masters at Barbados Thomas Beasly, John Gillespy, George R. Grand, and John Lawless

1830

Jan. 1	Dr. J. Vaughn Smith to A. H. Mechlin, Barbados
Jan. 4	James Lyon to A. H. Mechlin
Jan. 9	*The Niles Register*
Jan. ?	Charter Party with Michael Cavan & Co., Barbados

Jan 15 (?)	A. H. Mechlin to Branch, Barbados
Mar. 4	List of recaptured Africans arriving on the *Heroine*, Liberia
Mar. 20	Anonymous letter from Liberia on the arrival (printed in *African Repository and Colonial Journal #6*)
May 1	Court plea filed by Hernandez against the claim of Waters Smith
May 17	Accounting by Waters Smith for Smith vs. Hernandez
May 21	Branch to John MacPherson Berrier, Attorney General
Sept. 13	Branch to Waters Smith
unknown date (probably 1830)	Kendall to Branch

1831

May 13	John Boyle Acting Secretary of the Navy to Henry Ashton, Marshal of the US in the District of Columbia
May 13	Boyle to Gurley
May 19	Boyle to Ashton
May 19	Boyle to James Laurie, President of the Board of Managers of the Colonization Society, Washington
June 24	Levi Woodburn, Navy Dept., to Gurley
Sept. 30	Branch to Joseph Mechlin

1832

Mar.	Report by Joseph Mechlin
Mar. 11	*Liberia Herald* quoted in *African Repository and Colonial Journal*, Vol. IX

Apr.	Joseph Mechlin to Gurley
July	*African Repository and Colonial Journal* Vol. XIII
Sept.	*African Repository and Colonial Journal* Vol. IX

1833

Feb. 11	James C. Minor in Monrovia, Liberia to John Minor in Fredericksburg, Virginia
Jul (?)	*Liberia Herald* quoted in *African Repository and Colonial Journal*
Dec.	*African Repository and Colonial Journal*

1834

May 8	*The Philadelphian* quoted in *African Repository and Colonial Journal*
May	*African Repository and Colonial Journal*
June 2	Samson Caesar in Liberia to Henry F. Westfall in Virginia
Dec. 29	Journal of the House of Representatives

1835

Dec. 16	Journal of the House of Representatives

1836

Feb. 4	Report by the Committee on Claims on the petition of Samuel Sanderson, Washington (to accompany H.R. bill 274) (b)
Feb. 4	Journal of the House of Representatives

1837

Dec. 14	Reprint of the Report by the Committee on Claims on the petition of Sanderson (to accompany H.R. bill 16)(c)

1838

Dec. 11	American Colonization Society 22nd Annual Report

1839

May	*Liberia Herald*
July 30	Certification by Albion K. Parris, US Treasury Department (c)
Nov. 14	*New York Journal of Commerce*

1840

Nov. 25	Writ of attachment signed at Key West (c)

1841

May 3	Note on the writ of attachment by E. P. Hunk (?), Deputy Marshal, at Key West (c)

1843

Sept.	Census of the population of New Georgia, Liberia
Dec. 11	Albion K. Parris, Controller, Treasury Department, to David Henshaw, Secretary of the Navy

Items marked (a) were given to me by historian Jerry Wilkinson, from an inquiry he made to the National Archives, and I thank him for his contribution.

Item marked (b) was given to me by historian Jim Clupper, and it is much appreciated.

Items marked (c) were given to me by historian Tom Hambright, found in ancient files in the Key West library and I am grateful for the addition to the documentation.

Appendix Nine

Bounty List, HBM *Nimble*

Lt. Holland made this list of the ship's complement in Havana on December 31, 1827. The bounty paid to officers was 10 pounds for each liberated African.[262] The 38 crewmembers and eight Royal Marines aboard also received a bounty. When the name of the birthplace could not be determined in the script it is left blank.

Where Born	Name
Devonshire	Philip March
Liverpool	George King
Liverpool	John Peat
Glasgow	John Huld
	William Henry
	James Carter
Gravesend	John Day
Devonport	John Kastell
Westmoreland	Hugh Baird
Staffordshire	William Anderson
	Hugh Dunlivy
County Cork	John Mackay
	James Smith
Liverpool	William Smith
Cornwall	Thomas Rock
Gloucester	John Revell
Surrey	William Danney
Epex	Edward Kimmings
Shetland	Peter Swanson
Cove of Cork	Thomas Barry
Dublin	James Robinson

Plymouth	William Davis
Plymouth	Samuel Walters
Lymington	John Simmonds
Liverpool	John Jones
Liverpool	John Murray
Deal	John Brown
Jamaica	William Watson
Bristol	John P. Dodd
Portsmouth	Henry Nottingham
Cheshire	James Newby
	John Verpup
Kinkaldy	James Pringle
Sterling	Thomas Allison
Woolwich	John Gardener
Aberdeen	John Greenwater
Fareham	William Hawkins
Bridport	William Stodgell

Another list, apparently of officers aboard:

<u>Name</u>

G. W. Lewis
Andrew Beath
John Townsend
Charles G. Wilkie
Robert H. Elliot
G. B. Trevanion

The above list was signed by Holland and Robert H. Elliot (on the list), mate.

Royal Marines (Complement of 8)

Marines were soldiers specifically trained for maritime warfare, who served at sea.

Where Born	Name
Warwickshire	Thomas Bonner
Wilshire	Richard Macey
Somersetshire	Isaac Millet
Dorsetshire	William Dean
Liecester	Henry Scott
Liecester	William Clark
Norwich	William Cable
Somersetshire	William Ashford[263]

There were two other crewmen aboard the *Nimble* at the time of the capture of the *Guerrero* who do not appear on the above lists, for the log records on December 31, "Discharge G. Moore (SM) & J. Pinner to H. Schooner *Victor*." George Moore had been punished with 12 lashes on Christmas Day at Key West for "neglect of duty & disobedience of orders" according to the log.

Appendix Ten

Partial List of the Crew of the *Guerrero*

In 1820 the USS *Cyane* was off the coast of Africa capturing American-owned slave ships. This is from a letter written aboard that ship, probably by the commander, Edward Trenchard:

> The slave trade is carried on to a very great extent. There are probably not less than three hundred vessels on the coast, engaged in that traffic, each having two or three sets of papers. I sincerely hope Government have revised the law, giving us more authority. You have no idea how cruelly these poor creatures are treated by the monsters engaged in taking them from the coast.[264]

This is a partial list of the monsters of the *Guerrero*.

The list was made by Lt. Holland in Havana. Written on the form are: "Part of a crew of a Spanish slaver:...Spanish Slave Brig *Guerrero*" and "Spanish Government at Havana." An entry in the log of HBM *Nimble* on December 31, 1827, the same day this list was made, reads, "Discharged the prisoners."

Manuel Arcuntasa
Rafael Prieto
Antonio Fernandes
Jose C. Parages
Alexandro Errero
Lucas Cabado
Jose Axo [Antonio?] Otero

Isidre Baslida
Alexandro Lorenzo
Juan Bille
Andreo Fortinates
Raphael Ruys
Jose Martines
C. A. Benites
Francisco Lacirix
Manuel Ruy
Antonio Gonzales
Benito Calo
Antonio Vernande
Fillio Pelina[265]

Appendix Eleven

Accounting
of the 561 People in the *Guerrero*

Of the 561 people who had survived the Atlantic passage in the hold of the *Guerrero* at the time the ship approached Cuba only 92 ever again saw the shore of Africa.

In the hold[266]	561
Missing after the wrecking (drowned or crushed by the masts) [267]	41
Survivors	520
Hijacked to Cuba Onboard the *Florida*[268]	146
Hijacked to Cuba Onboard the *Thorn*[269]	252
Total enslaved in Cuba	398
Taken aboard the *Surprize*[270]	122
Died before the *Surprize* arrived at Key West[271]	1
Died at Key West[272]	6
Taken by Capt. Doane aboard the *Marion*[273]	1
Known to have died at St. Augustine, probably includes the death at Mala Compra[274](To Oct. 27, 1828)	3
African interpreter released to go to Havana[275]	1
Died in care at Ross residence, Jacksonville[276]	1
Died in Florida of yaws after the departure of the	

Washington's Barge[277]	1
Also kept from boarding due to yaws,[278] possibly "John," the last African (There is a possibility that "John" was the boy with Capt. Doane.)	1 ·
Subtotal	15
Boarded the *Washington's Barge*[279]	100
Subtotal	115
Unaccounted for from 122 people, probably deaths between Oct. 28, 1828 and Sept. 30, 1829	7
The 100 recaptive Africans were joined on the voyage by six Kroomen returning to their coastal homes.[280]	
Died on the voyage to Liberia[281] (Five had died before reaching Barbados.[282])	9
Arrived at Liberia[283]	91
John, liberated African, sent to Liberia June, 1831[284]	1
Total people from the *Guerrero* to arrive at Liberia	92

Endnotes

Abbreviations:

PRO   Public Record Office in London
NA   National Archives in Washington

[1] Names of the people who arrived on the brig *Heroine* in Tom W. Shick, *Emigrants to Liberia 1820 to 1843, An Alphabetical Listing*, Liberian Studies Research Working Paper No. 2, Liberian Studies Association in America, Inc. (1971) and "Information relative to the operations of the United States squadron on the west coast of Africa...Brig *Heroine*'s company arrived at Monrovia March 4, 1830" in 28th Congress, 2d. Doc. 150, serial 458.

[2] See Chapter 14.

[3] "A Few Facts Respecting the American Colonization Society, and the Colony at Liberia" (circular), American Colonization Society (1830).

[4] Twenty-Second American Colonization Society Report, December 11, 1838.

[5] Hugh Thomas wrote the yearly number of Africans shipped to the New World in the 1820s was 60,000 to 70,000. See his book *The Slave Trade, The Story of the Atlantic Slave Trade: 1440-1870* (1997), p. 650.

[6] Thomas, p. 11.

[7] Dr. Madeleine H. Burnside, Director of the Mel Fisher Maritime Heritage Society wrote in the *Navigator* (the Society's newsletter), May, 2005 the following: "We are very sorry to have to say goodbye to our wonderful assistant curator...[she] has been with us for sixteen months and has done a great job researching different aspects of the collection - particularly the religious artifacts. She has done a lot of writing both for the newsletter and exhibits, which has been immensely valuable to us. She also went to sea with the archaeological team in their survey of the merchant slaver *Guerrero* and assisted in documenting the site. We will really miss her cheery countenance and intellectual shine, not to mention her skills!" So, the *Guerrero* had been found? Why no other publicity than this if the wreck had been found? I contacted Brenda S. Altmeier, Florida Keys National Marine Sanctuary, Key Largo, as the group was working under a permit from that office and asked if I could get reports

that must have been filed in her office on the discovery (e-mail, Swanson to Altmeier, May 25, 2005), as well as Brenda Lanzendorf, Archaeologist, Biscayne National Park, near or in the area that I believe the *Guerrero* should be found. Altmeier replied as follows: "To date no positive identification has been established regarding the location(s) of the wreck or wreckage materials associated with the shipwreck *Guerrero*. Ms. Brown must have been part of the team on board the survey vessel performing mag work this past summer. The vessel was provided by RPM Nautical and several individuals from the MFMHS [Mel Fisher Maritime Heritage Society] participated during the summer survey sessions. Documentation of the magnetometer anomaly hits were performed." (e-mail, Altmeier to Swanson, May 25, 2005)After I received that the May 25, 2005 e-mails between Dr. Burnside and I were quite lively, with her affirming what she had written to be a fact. I knew that the team that had been looking for the wreck hadn't surveyed the area miles away where I believe it to be (even though I had provided team member Denis Trelewicz with a marked up map of the south end of Pacific Reef in 2001, as well as having urged him by phone twice in 2003 to consider magging more northerly than the Turtle Rocks area, where the the magging work was being performed). Later, on June 16, 2005, Archaeologist Lanzendorf and I were taking questions from the audience after the showing of the documentary, The *Guerrero* Project, at the Historical Museum of Southern Florida in Miami. One member of the audience asked "How do you know the *Guerrero* hasn't already been found?" Lanzendorf's reply was long, about rechecking some known sites, but there was not ever an indication in her reply that the *Guerrero* had been found.

[8] Canning never saw this correspondence, for he died Aug. 8, and it was received in London on Oct. 7.

[9] The *Indagadora* succeeded in landing her cargo in Cuba. See "List of vessels which have returned from the coast of Africa and have succeeded in landing cargoes of slaves in the neighborhood of Havana during the year 1827" in PRO, file reference FO 84/80.

[10] PRO. House of Commons Sessional Papers, Accounts and Papers (1828), XXVI, file reference ZHC 1/914, No. 113, p. 143.

[11] David R. Murray, *Odious Commerce, Britain, Spain, and the Abolition of the Cuban Slave Trade* (1980), p. 77.

[12] Thomas, p. 639.

[13] Thomas, p. 636.

[14] Murray, p. 80.

[15] See my paper, "Slave Ships at the Florida Keys" for details of British slave ships known to have wrecked at the Florida Keys: the *Henrietta Marie* in 1700, the *Nassau* in 1741, and the *Fly* in 1789. (It is unpublished, but was distributed at the Florida Keys Maritime History Conference, Key West, May, 2000. I may have given a copy to the Key West library.) The wrecks of the *Nassau* and the *Fly* have not been discovered. The *slaver Fly* should not be confused with HMS *Fly*, which wrecked at the Keys in 1805.

[16] Luis Martinez-Fernandez, *Fighting Slavery in the Caribbean, The Life and Times of a British Family in Nineteenth-Century Havana* (1998), p. 46.

[17] PRO. Henry T. Kilbee and W. S. Macleay to Captain General Francisco Dionisio Vives, Havana, Dec. 31, 1827, file reference FO 84/80.

[18] After the wrecking of the slaver Capt. John H. Sawyer of Key West carried the news written by "a correspondent" to Pensacola, where, it was related in the *Pensacola Gazette* of Feb. 8, 1828, that "the Spanish brig *Guerrero*, (alias, *San Jose*)..." The former name of the *Guerrero* was surely provided by the British at Key West, learned from Kilbee and Macleay's communication.

[19] *Church Missionary Intelligencer,* vol. VII, p. 67-71.

[20] James Montgomery, James Grahame, and E. Benger, *Poems on the Abolition of the Slave Trade* (1809). The full name of the poem is "Africa Delivered; Or, The Slave Trade Abolished. A Poem."

[21] *Report of Mr. Kennedy, of Maryland, from the Committee on Commerce of the House of Representatives of the United States on the African Slave Trade* (1843, reprinted 1971), p. 976.

[22] Thomas, p. 653.

[23] Thomas, p. 653.

[24] PRO. Commissioners Henry T. Kilbee and W. S. Macleay, Havana, Jan. 3, 1828, file reference FO 84/80, p. 20.

[25] NA. United States v. Schooner *Feniz*, Sept., 1831, in 230/1/33/2, Box 4. This is an appeal by the Spanish "owners" of the "slaves" that includes the papers of 1830, the year of the capture of the *Feniz*.

[26] W. E. F. Ward, *The Royal Navy and the Slave Trade* (1970), pp. 134-135.

[27] *Savannah Georgian*, January 21, 1828. The number does not agree with the log of the *Nimble*, which states "8 long 12 pounders and 6 medium 12 pounders."

[28] *Savannah Georgian*, January 21, 1828.

[29] M. H. Stacey to D. B. Stacey in Philadelphia, *Crusader*, Key West, May 2, 1860 (transcript), State and Local History Collection, Monroe County Public Library at Key West.

[30] NA. Lt. Commander T. Augustus Craven to Secretary of the Navy Isaac Touchey, June 8, 1860.

[31] Robert Walsh, *Notices of Brazil in 1828 and 1829* (1831).

[32] PRO. Log of HBM *Monkey*, June 27, 1829.

[33] The *Lapwing* was 107 tons. The vessel and her captain, Thomas Kennedy, were regulars in the domestic slave trade (legal in American law at the time) from Baltimore to New Orleans. At the time of the boarding Kennedy had only two enslaved people aboard; Kitty, age 40, and Lucy, age 30, their owner/shipper was Henry Thompson. The *Lapwing* had left Baltimore Nov. 28 and Savannah Dec. 14. She arrived in New Orleans on Dec. 23, 1827. In a voyage earlier in the year (Baltimore departure Feb. 16, arrival in New Orleans, Mar. 15) 50 enslaved people were aboard. There are records of an 1822 voyage, same ports, with 61 aboard, and an 1833 voyage by slave ship captain Kennedy in the *Ulysses*, same ports, with 14 enslaved aboard. See Ralph Clayton, *Cash for Blood, The Baltimore to New Orleans Domestic Slave Trade* (2002), pp. 537, 543, 633, 638. For the date of departure from Savannah see the *Charleston Mercury*, Dec. 17, 1827.

[34] Unnamed correspondent in Key West to *The American and Commercial Daily Advertiser* (Baltimore), dated Dec. 26, 1827, printed Jan. 18, 1828. The *Lapwing* incident is also recorded in the log of the *Nimble*, but the *Reuben Ross* chase is not.

[35] PRO. File reference ADM 1/3322.

[36] PRO. Bounty list prepared by Lt. Edward Holland, plus two men discharged to HBM *Victor*.

[37] *Pensacola Gazette*, February 8, 1828.

[38] *Savannah Georgian*, January 21, 1828.

[39] Howard I. Chapelle, *History of American Sailing Ships*, pp. 161-162.

[40] *Savannah Georgian*, January 21, 1828.

[41] *Pensacola Gazette*, February 8, 1828.

[42] *Savannah Georgian* (quoting the *Charleston Courier*), Jan. 21, 1828.

[43] PRO. Deposition of John Whalton, commander of the lightboat *Caesar*

at Bason Bank, the Florida Reef, Foreign Office: America Series II: General Correspondence. 1828 Jan - Mar 4, file reference FO 5/237, Folio 21.

[44] Letter quoted in *The Royal Gazette*, January 5, 1828.

[45] Letter to the editor of *The American and Commercial Daily Advertiser* from Key West, Dec. 26, 1827, correspondent's name not noted, published Jan. 14, 1828.

[46] *Niles Register* (Baltimore), Feb. 2, 1828.

[47] *Royal Gazette* (Nassau), Jan. 5, 1828.

[48] The log and *Pensacola Gazette*, February 8, 1828.

[49] Captains M. D. Ricker, W. Rollins and David Dixon Porter at various times complained that although the lightship was supposed to be displaying two flashing white lights 30 and 40 feet above the sea, visible for 12 miles, the lights were "scarcely discernible from the outer ridge of Carysfort reef, which is four to five miles distant," [Porter] and the captain of the mail-passenger steamer *Isabel*, making twice-monthly voyages between Charleston and Key West, said the lightship was "a poor thing...cannot depend on it at all." Thomas W. Taylor, *Lore of the Reef Lights: Life in the Florida Keys* (2005).

[50] NA. Protest taken by Richard Fitzpatrick given by John Morrison, Samuel Sanderson, Charles Grover, and John Walker, at Key West, January 1, 1828. SD, Misc. Letters C45.

[51] *A Description of the Windward Passage and Gulf of Florida* (London, 1739), p. 11-13.

[52] PRO. Deposition of William Wright, attached to Kilbee & Macleay to the Earl of Dudley, file reference FO 84/80.

[53] NA. Protest, *Thorn* against *Guerrero*, SD, Misc. Letters, C45.

[54] William Marvin, *Treatise on the Law of Wreck and Salvage* (1858), p. 131. It is unknown whether the wreckers requested a salvage fee on the Africans from Lt. Holland. They may have thought better of it, as the Africans saved were not under the control of the British, but were under the control of the Cubans and, those in Key West, the Americans.

[55] PRO. Deposition of Samuel Sanderson, master of the sloop *Surprize*, FO 5/236-237, folio 217.

[56] NA. Protest taken by Richard Fitzpatrick given by John Morrison, Samuel Sanderson, Charles Grover, and John Walker, at Key West, January 1, 1828, SD, Misc. Letters, C45.

[57] See the list of 10 smacks built at Essex in the 1830s in Howard I. Chapelle, *The American Fishing Schooners 1825-1935* (1973), p. 59.

[58] This might have been standard practice, though. The log of HBM Monkey (PRO), June 17, 1829 records, upon the capture of the slaver *Midas*, "People putting prize to rights throwing overboard all the shot, powder, arms & spiking the guns."

[59] PRO. Holland to Charles R. Vaughan, written at Havana, Jan. 1, 1828, FO 5/236, folio 150.

[60] NA. Report of P. C. Fuller, Committee of Claims, Feb. 4, 1836 in House of Representatives Report No. 4, 25th Congress, 2d Session, 1837.

[61] PRO. Deposition of John Whalton, January 7, 1828, FO 5/236.

[62] PRO. Deposition of Charles Grover, Jan. 7, 1828, FO 5/236, folio 213.

[63] PRO. Deposition of Nathaniel Grover (should read "Glover" - as Andrea Cordani remarked in the tape on this error, "I think the clerk has gotten himself into a bit of a mess here, Gail."), Jan. 7, 1828, FO 5/236, folio 21.

[64] It was common for slave ships to have hired doctors onboard. For some accounts of slave ship surgeons see James A. Rawley, *The Transatlantic Slave Trade* (1981), p. 296-297.

[65] Deposition of Nathaniel Glover.

[66] In 1827 the population of Cuba was 704,487, with 311,051 white, 106,494 free colored, and 286,942 enslaved. See *Resumen del censo de la pobacion de la isla de Cuba* (Havana: Impr. del Gobierno, 1842), p. 19.

[67] Thomas Randall at Havana in 1824 noted this in his journal entry on September 29, confirming what Conneau wrote: "A large Spanish brig arrived in ballast supposed to have been to the coast of Africa to have landed a cargo of African slaves on the coast of this island." Papers of Thomas Randall, Maryland Historical Society Library, Baltimore.

[68] Theophilus Conneau, *A Slaver's Log Book or 20 Years' Residence in Africa* (1976), p. 87-89.

[69] Joseph Bethel, pilot, and John Cargo.

[70] *Charleston Mercury*, Jan. 10, 1828.

[71] PRO. Deposition of Samuel Sanderson, January 7, 1828, FO 5/236-237, folio 217.

[72] Deposition of Nathaniel Glover.

[73] From Holland to Pinkney, Dec. 25, 1827, (PRO, FO 5/236-237, folio 164) "I...early the next morning...engaged with the master of the *Surprize* to convey the negroes to Key West. This I was obliged to do in consequence of my having a very small quantity of water aboard, and none to be procured in the vicinity. Upon these grounds I consider the negroes as under the protection of the British government...." Holland states this again in his letter of Jan. 1 to Charles R. Vaughan (folio 150), "In the morning, some American wreckers appeared, the masters of who I engaged to take the negroes on board, and convey them to Key West, they having refused to go to the Havana." Of course the wreckers intended on getting their "arbitration" award at Key West, and were bound there whether Holland paid them to go there or not!

[74] PRO. Deposition of John Walker, January 7, 1828, FO 5/236, folio 221.

[75] Trade goods. Also used for barter was rum and tobacco.

[76] PRO. Deposition of John Morrison, January 7, 1828, FO 5/236, folio 219.

[77] NA. Protest, *Thorn* of *Guerrero*. taken by Algernon S. Thurston at Key West Dec. 26, 1827, SD Misc. Letters C45.

[78] *American and Commercial Daily Advertiser* (Baltimore), Jan. 14, 1828.

[79] Census taken by Collector of Customs (William Pinkney) Feb. 25, 1828 shows 216 Free White Males, Permanent Residents 100 Free White Males, 8 mo. (Fishing) [Mostly Residents of Connecticut], 49 Free White Females, 21 Free Black Males, 18 Free Black Females, 17 Slaves. The *Guerrero* people were in residence the day the census was taken, yet were not noted at all in the figures.

[80] Thomas W. Taylor, *The Key West Lighthouse, A Light in Paradise* (2004), p. 10. This lighthouse was not the lighthouse seen today at Key West nor even on the same site. The first lighthouse collapsed in the horrific hurricane at Key West in 1846.

[81] I have a book in preparation on this subject: *Mystic, Ct. Seafarers at Key West*.

[82] Deposition of John Earl (document 28, pp. 3-4) in Gail Swanson, compiler, "The Case of Ten New York Marine Insurance Companies vs. Charles Johnson, Wrecker of the Florida Keys in the Matter of the ship *Hercules* grounded off Key Largo in 1825," binder, Monroe County Public Library at Key West and Islamorada and at P. K. Yonge Library

of Florida History, University of Florida. This is my transcription of American Insurance Company and others vs. Charles Johnson, NA, Northeast Region, M919, Roll 26.

[83] NA, Department of State, Misc. Letters, January. - March 1828, M179, Roll 66.

[84] The Act of Congress passed March 3, 1825, contained this wording:If any ship or vessel shall, after passing respect, be engaged or employed in carrying or transporting any property whatsoever, taken from any wreck, from the sea, or from any of the Keys or shoals, within the jurisdiction of the United States on the coast of Florida to any foreign port or place, every such ship or vessel so engaged, and employed together with her tackle and furniture, shall be wholly forfeited and may be seized and condemned in any court of the United States or territories thereof having a competent jurisdiction.

[85] PRO. E. Holland to Vice-Admiral of the White, Charles E. Fleming, Jan. 18, 1828, file reference FO 5/237, folio 194.

[86] PRO. FO 5/237, folio 170.

[87] *American and Commercial Daily Advertiser* (Baltimore), Jan. 18, 1828.

[88] NA. SD Misc. Letters C45, page 0090.

[89] NA. Lt. Holland to "Gentlemen, " December 17, 1827, SD Misc. Letters C45, p. 0090.

[90] PRO. FO 5/237, folio 231.

[91] An incident onboard the *Nimble* while at Key West was the whipping of George Moore on Christmas Day. One wonders if the Africans could have heard this man's terrifying screams of pain and if so what their reactions were.

[92] PRO. FO 5/237, folio 194.

[93] Thomas, p. 607. See also Luis Martinez-Fernandez, *Fighting Slavery in the Caribbean, The Life and Times of a British Family in Nineteenth-Century Havana* (1998), p. 50, for the lives in virtual slavery of Escolastica and Marcelino Urrutia, both Africans freed from slave ships in 1828 and Arthur F. Corwin, *Spain and the Abolition of Slavery in Cuba, 1817-1886*, pp. 40-42.

[94] *Savannah Georgian*, January 21, 1828.

[95] PRO, John Morrison, Samuel Sanderson, Charles Grover, John Walker to Henry Clay, January 5, 1828, FO 5/237, folio 20.

[96] Waters Smith, Marshal's Office, Eastern District of Florida, to Richard Rush, Secretary of the Treasury, St. Augustine, April 2, 1828. The letter is printed in Document 262, House of Representatives, 20th Congress, 1st Session, "Africans at Key West. Message from the President of the United States Relative to the Disposition of The Africans Landed at Key West from a Stranded Spanish Vessel, April 30, 1828."

[97] The identity of the deputy is in Waters Smith's affadavit sworn before Thomas F. Cornell, March 11, 1828.

[98] *Savannah Georgian*, May 14, 1827, p. 2, c. 4 (courtesy of historian John Viele). The article reads, in part, "Key West - There have been strange doings at this Island. Everything however has been kept very snug until lately, when learning the consequences of further delay, some disclosures have been made which induced a visit from the Marshal, in order to pay his personal respects to about 60 individuals." A later article in the same paper on July 21 gives more information; "Pinkney says the Marshal came to Key West to arrest the masters of eight fishing vessels for making a voyage to Havana without a clearance."

[99] NA. Waters Smith to Samuel L. Southard, Washington City, October 27, 1828, Misc. Letters to the Secretary of the Navy, RG 45, M124, Roll 116.

[100] For reference to the storchouses see Gail Swanson, compiler, "The Case of Ten New York Marine Insurance Companies vs. Charles Johnson," document 18. For reference to the barracks see Walter C. Maloney, *A Sketch of the History of Key West* (1876), p. 9.

[101] Miscellaneous Florida Manuscripts Box 13, P. K. Yonge Library of Florida History, University of Florida. I am indebted to Dinizulu Gene Tinnie for sharing his transcription of the document which we both found in our separate research..

[102] NA. Thomas F. Cornell, Deputy Collector of the Customs for the District of St. Augustine to Richard Rush, March 15th, 1828.

[103] I am currently preparing a book on the events of 1860 and my documentation and my discovery of the African Cemetery on Higgs Beach.

[104] *Charleston Mercury*, February 4, 1828.

[105] See Appendix Ten. The *Nimble* arrived in Havana on Dec. 30 and left January 2.

[106] PRO. Havana Commissioners Kilbee & Macleay to the Earl of Dudley, and attachments including the testimony of William Wright, in FO 84/80.

[107] PRO. Kilbee & Macleay to the Earl of Dudley, FO 84/80.

[108] Thomas, p. 640.

[109] PRO. Franco. Dionisio Vives to Kilbee & Macleay in FO 84/80.

[110] *The Royal Gazette*, January 5, 1828.

[111] PRO. Log of HBM *Nimble* January 15, 1828. File reference ADM 1/3322.

[112] PRO. Holland to Pinkney, Dec. 25, 1827, FO 5/236-237, folio 164.

[113] PRO. FO 5/237, folio 219.

[114] From a message board posting with no authorship - possibly by Beverly K. Mott, RootsWeb.com, posted March 22, 2004.

[115] PRO. Charles Edmonston and John Geddes to the Honorable Henry Clay, Secretary of State, Jan. 25, 1828, file reference FO 5/236, folio 197.

[116] Thomas, p. 600.

[117] NA. Letters from Collectors, Key West, M-178, Roll 38.

[118] NA. Waters Smith to Secretary of the Treasury Richard Rush, February 8, 1828.

[119] PRO. Henry Clay to Charles Vaughan, Feb. 18, 1828, file reference FO 5/237, folio 178.

[120] PRO. Henry Clay to Charles Vaughan, Feb. 18, 1828, FO 5/237, folio 178.

[121] Luis Rafael Arana and Albert Manucy, "The Building of Castillo de San Marcos" (booklet) (1977).

[122] Kathryn Hall Proby, *John James Audubon* (1974), p. 17.

[123] NA. Cornell to Rush, Doc. No. 262, "Papers relating to the introduction of slaves into the port of St. Augustine."

[124] NA. Miscellaneous Letters Received by the Secretary of the Navy, RG 45, M124, Roll 115, p. 79.

[125] Jane Landers, *Black Society in Spanish Florida* (1999), Appendix II, "African Imports into Spanish Florida, 1784-1821," p. 276.

[126] The schooner *Laurel*, alias *Juanita*, brought 25 Africans from St. Thomas in 1804 and 10 more in a later voyage that same year, from Havana, the *Pez* or *Peje*, Capt. Joel Dunn, brought 16 Africans from Mozambique for Kingsley in 1806, the *Esther* arrived in Havana where

Kingsley sold 43 Africans and purchased 3 more from another slaver and imported them into Florida on the same *Esther*, and the *Industry* brought to Florida 10 enslaved from Georgia for or by Kingsley. See Jane Landers, *Black Society in Spanish Florida*, p. 276 for the *Peje*, Daniel Schafer, *Anna Kingsley* (1997), p. 11 for the *Esther*, and American State Papers, Public Lands, Vol. 4 for the *Laurel*, *Pez* from Charleston (Lander's source is written *Peje*, coming from Mozambique) the *Esther* and the *Industry*, cited in Philip S. May, "Zephaniah Kingsley, Nonconformist (1765-1843)," *Florida Historical Quarterly*, Vol. 23, Issue 3.

[127] Jean B. Stephens, "Zephaniah Kingsley and the Recaptured Africans" in *El Escribano*, Vol. 15 (1978).

[128] St. John's County Court Records, St. Augustine Historical Society Library.

[129] NA. Waters Smith to Joseph M. White, St. Augustine, April 2, 1828, RG 45, M124, Roll 114, p. 16.

[130] St. Augustine Historical Society Library, St. John's County Court Records.

[131] Conversation with Ted Payne at the St. Augustine Historical Society Library, April 21, 2004.

[132] Ted M. Payne and Patricia C. Griffin, "Preliminary Archaeological Investigations at the Joseph Martin Hernandez Mala Compra Plantation Settlement at Bings Landing County Park, Flagler County, Florida," June 30, 1999 (unpublished), St. Augustine Historical Society Library.

[133] Griffin to Swanson, e-mail, May 25, 2004.

[134] NA. Waters Smith to Southard, October 27, 1828, Misc. Letters Rec'd by the Secretary of the Navy.

[135] President John Quincy Adams' diary 11 November 1828 - 24 June 1828, microfilm Roll 40 pp. 500, 501, 505, 506, Richter Library, University of Miami.

[136] Journal of the House, United States Government Publications Serial set, 20th Congress, December 3, 1827 - March 3, 1829, p. 650 (microcard).

[137] Howard Jones, *Mutiny on the Amistad* (1987), pp. 45, 81.

[138] NA. Samuel L. Southard to Waters Smith, August 7, 1828, Misc. Letters Sent by the Secretary of the Navy.

[139] NA. RG 45, M124, Roll 114, p. 16.

[140] NA. Waters Smith to Samuel L. Southard, Nov. 1, 1828, Secretary of the Navy, Miscellaneous Letters Received.

[141] NA. Secretary of the Navy Samuel L. Southard to Waters Smith, Nov. 18, 1828, Miscellaneous Letters sent by the Secretary of the Navy.

[142] NA. Secretary of the Navy Samuel L. Southard to John Hanson, Nov. 20, 1828, Miscellaneous Letters sent by the Secretary of the Navy.

[143] NA. Senate Document 1, 20th Congress, Second Session, p. 127. (microcard)

[144] NA. Journal of the House, US Serial Set No. 1183, 20th Congress, Second Session, Dec. 1, 1828 - March 3, 1829, p. 152 (microcard).

[145] NA. Secretary of the Navy Samuel L. Southard to Dr. Richard Randall, Jan. 24, 1829.

[146] NA. RG 45, M124, Roll 121. This letter is indexed incorrectly as dated October 22, 1829, which is indeed the postmark. It is an April 22 letter, however.

[147] NA. Branch to Waters Smith, May 8, 1829, Misc. Letters Sent by the Secretary of the Navy.

[148] NA. Branch to Miles King, Navy Agent, Norfolk, June 15, 1829. McPhail and Robert Soutter had transported 142 recaptured Africans, 120 of them from the *Antelope/General Ramirez* in the *Norfolk*. See their Charter Party in NA, Correspondence of the Secretary of the Navy Relating to African Colonization, M205, Roll 2, 1819-1844. The payment by the US for that voyage was $28 for those over ten, and half price ($14) for those under ten. McPhail had also sailed to the same coast with agents Joseph Andrus and Christian Wiltberger, Ephrium Bacon, Jonathan B. Winn, and 33 African American emigrants in the *Nautilus* on January 23, 1821.

[149] Typescript, "The Patriot War, A Contemporaneous Letter," the letter dated at St. Marys, April 1, 1818, the original noted as "in the Bureau of Index and Archives, Department of State, Washington, D. C." in 1927, The Amelia Island Museum of History, Fernandina Beach, Florida.

[150] West Publishing, *The Federal cases: comprising cases argued and determined in the Circuit and District courts of the United States from the earliest times to the beginning of the Federal reporter* (1894-1897), Case No. 18,269a, p. 1029.

[151] Thomas, p. 616.

[152] Square 18, Lot 5. Files of the The Amelia Island Museum of History.

[153] NA. Misc. Letters Rec'd by the Secretary of the Navy, RG 45, M124, Roll 120.

[154] See articles in *Freedom's Journal*. Historian Jacqueline Bacon gives these examples: "Coloured Children," Jan. 18, 1828, "Kidnapping," Aug. 8, 1828, and "Shocking Occurrence," Dec. 5, 1828.

[155] NA. Waters Smith to John Branch, Fernandina, Amelia Island, Aug. 28, 1829 Misc. Letters Received by the Secretary of the Navy, RG 45, M124, Roll 120, letter 77.

[156] *Florida Herald* (St. Augustine), Sept. 16, 1829.

[157] The census is on microfilm at the St. Augustine Historical Society Library, St. Augustine, Florida.

[158] NA. Branch to Barron, Sept. 19, 1829, Misc. Letters Sent by the Secretary of the Navy.

[159] C. C. Mettler, *History of Medicine* (1947), pp. 635-636 for the latent period. Dr. William M. Straight of Miami, a physician and historian of medicine in Florida, could find no mention of yaws in Florida in his private library.

[160] NA. Branch to Smith, October 30, 1829, Misc. Letters Sent by the Secretary of the Navy.

[161] *Niles' Register*, Jan. 9, 1830, p. 326.

[162] St. Johns County Court Records, Civil action in 1834, St. Augustine Historical Society Library, Location 131-26. The action is foreclosure on the residence after Smith's death.

[163] NA. Mechlin to Branch, with enclosures (correspondence between he and Governor Lyon and the survey of the vessel, among the enclosures), January 15, 1830 Misc. Letters Rec'd by the Secretary of the Navy. RG 45. The arrival date of the *Heroine* is from *The African Repository and Colonial Journal*, vol. 6 (1830), p. 49-51.

[164] Clarence Edwin Carter, compiler, *The Territorial Papers of the United States*, Vol. XXII (1956), p. 568.

[165] Carter, pp. 563-564.

[166] Biographical file of Thomas Douglas, St. Augustine Historical Society Library.

[167] Senate Executive Journal, 1829-1837, per website "American Memory."

[168] Mars Lucas to Townsend Heaton, written onboard the brig *Liberia* at

Caldwell, Liberia, March 12, 1830, The Lucas-Heaton Letters, collection of the Loudoun Museum, Leesburg, Virginia.

[169] Claude A. Clegg, III, *The Price of Liberty, African Americans and the Making of Liberia* (2004), p. 81.

[170] Alfred Brockenbrough Williams, *The Liberian Exodus. An Account of the Voyage of the First Emigrants in the Bark "Azor" and their reception at Monrovia, with a description of Liberia - Its Customs, Romances and Prospects* (1878), University of North Carolina at Chapel Hill Electronic Edition (2000).

[171] Mars Lucas to Townsend Heaton, Caldwell, Liberia, June 19, 1830, The Lucas-Heaton Letters, collection of the Loudoun Museum, Leesburg, Virginia.

[172] Website, www.pages.prodigy.net/jkess3/Antelope.htm.

[173] Clegg, p. 93.

[174] *The African Repository and Colonial Journal*, v. VI, 1830, pp. 49-51.

[175] Clegg, pp. 104-105.

[176] *The African Repository*, vol. IX, 1832, p. 158.

[177] *The African Repository*, vol. XIII, 1832, p. 135.

[178] *The African Repository*, Dec., 1833.

[179] *The African Repository*, vol. XI, May, 1834, p. 90.

[180] Samson Ceasar to Henry F. Westfall, University of Virginia Library Electronic Text Center.

[181] Jesse Lucas to Friends, Caldwell, April 24, 1836, The Lucas-Heaton Letters, collection of the Loudoun Museum, Leesburg, Virginia.

[182] I have yet to find the connection between John Russwurm and the *Guerrero* survivor Caesar Russwurm.

[183] Janice Borzendowski, *John Russwurm* (1989) pp. 64, 79.

[184] *Report of Mr. Kennedy, of Maryland, from the Committee on Commerce of the House of Representatives of the United States on the African Slave Trade* (1843, reprinted 1971), p. 896.

[185] The report is in *Report of Mr. Kennedy, of Maryland,* p. 904.

[186] *Report of Mr. Kennedy, of Maryland*, p. 898.

[187] Tom W. Shick, *Behold the Promised Land, A History of Afro-American Settler Society in Nineteenth-Century Liberia* (1977), p. 67.

[188] "Information relative to the operations of the United States squadron on the west coast of Africa, the condition of the American colonies there, and the commerce of the United States therewith," 28th Congress, 2d. Session, Senate Document 250, serial 458. It is transcribed at www.ccharity.com/liberia/newgeorgiacensus.htm.

[189] Shick, *Behold the Promised Land,* p. 68.

[190] Surely "Kinsley" is too close to "Kingsley" to come to any other conclusion.

[191] Horatio Bridge, Nathaniel Hawthorne, ed., *Journal of an African Cruiser* (1853), p. 43.

[192] Bridge, p. 98.

[193] The article is printed on the "Exploring *Amistad* at Mystic Seaport" website under "Library" then "Correspondence of the Journal of Commerce," www.amistad.mysticseaport.org.

[194] A letter from Henry Clay to Charles Edmonston on Feb. 9, 1828, in reply to his and Geddes' letter of Jan. 25 with the wreckers' memorials has not been found in the archives, although its existence is known for it was referred to in a March 31 letter from Edmonston to Clay.

[195] Bryan Riggs, *Historic Homes, Charleston, So. Carolina* (1993), p. 86-87.

[196] NA. Southard to Edmonston, May 21, 1828, Misc. Letters Sent by the Secretary of the Navy.

[197] PRO. Fleming to Vaughan, April 16, 1828, FO 5/327, folio 192. The description of H.M.S. *Barham* is from Thomas Foster, *The Postal History of Jamaica 1662-1860.*

[198] Gold was used to buy slaves, especially from slave traders of the interior of Africa.

[199] NA. SD, Misc. Letters, C45.

[200] NA. Waters Smith statement sworn before Thomas F. Cornell, March 11, 1828.

[201] PRO. Testimony of William Wright enclosed in Havana Commissioners Kilbee & Macleay to the Earl of Dudly, FO 84/80.

[202] Report by the Committee on Claims [by P. C. Fuller] on the petition of Samuel Sanderson, to accompany H. R. bill no. 274, 24th Congress, lst session, House Reports, 24th Congress, lst session, I., No. 168; House Reports, 25th Congress 2nd session l, No. 4; Treasury Department, Fourth Auditor's Office certification, July 30, 1839, No. 5647;

Summons, US to the Marshal of the Superior Court of the Southern District of Florida, November 25, 1840 and return of the writ, same reference, State and Local History Room, Monroe County Library at Key West.

[203] The prize, or bounty, list was apparently made by Lt. Holland on Dec. 31, 1827, and completed by the Admiralty on June 29, 1832. See PRO, ADM 37/8414.

[204] John Viele, notes on log of US Revenue Cutter *Marion*, collection of the author via John Viele.

[205] PRO. File reference ADM 51/3306. The log refers to "HMS *Nimble*" and is entitled "HMS *Monkey*." The *Christian Advocate and Journal and Zion's Herald* (New York), July 24, 1829 refers to "HBM" *Monkey*.

[206] W. E. F. Ward, *The Royal Navy and the Slavers* (1970), p. 137.

[207] Notes on *Nimble* and *Monkey* from Dinizulu Gene Tinnie, citing as his source William Laird Clowes, *The Royal Navy: A History from Earliest Times to the Present*, Vol. VI (1966), p. 268.

[208] Richard Kerwin MacMaster, *The United States, Great Britain and the Suppression of the Cuban Slave Trade 1835-1860* (1968 dissertation, Georgetown University), p. 16.

[209] David R. Murray, *Odious Commerce, Britain, Spain, and the Abolition of the Cuban Slave Trade* (1980), p. 279.

[210] Howard I. Chapelle, *History of American Sailing Ships* (1935) pp. 161-162.

[211] Richard Kerwin MacMaster, *The United States, Great Britain and the Suppression of the Cuban Slave Trade 1835-1860* p. 17 and W. P. Gosset, *The Lost Ships of the Royal Navy, 1793-1900* (1986), p. 105.

[212] The American Colonization Society, *Annual Report*, pp. 33-36.

[213] Over the ship's side.

[214] Bernard Romans was the fun-loving surveyor.

[215] I am indebted to Chuck Hayes for questioning my orginal transcriptions of "1/8 W." and 1/8 E."

[216] PRO. Deposition of John Morrison, FO 5/236, folio 219.

[217] Thomas W. Taylor, *Florida's Territorial Lighthouses, 1824-1845* (1995), p. 259.

[218] Tom Hambright at the Key West library made this determination.

[219] This item was copied in Savannah by John and Pam Viele and transcribed and given to me by them.

[220] Thomas W. Taylor, *Lore of the Reef Lights; Life in the Florida Keys.* (2005)

[221] From the summary of a log transcript given to me by historian John Viele. I have lost the cover page with the name of the vessel.

[222] PRO. Log of HBN *Nimble*, December 19, 1827, ADM 1/3322.

[223] PRO. Deposition of Charles Grover, FO 5/236, folio 213.

[224] PRO. Deposition of Charles Grover.

[225] NA., Northeast Region. American Insurance Company and others vs. Charles Johnson, M919, Roll 26 (under the name of the vessel, the *Hercules*).

[226] Journal of Hiram Clift aboard the *Gallant*, April 14, 1825 entry, G. W. Blunt White Library, Mystic Seaport, Mystic, Ct.

[227] Paul David Nelson, *General James Grant, Scottish Soldier and Royal Governor of East Florida* (1993), p. 60.

[228] Jane Landers, *Black Society in Spanish Florida* (1999), p. 157.

[229] Jane Landers, *Black Society in Spanish Florida* (1999), p. 157 and Appendix 9, "Slave Imports into Florida, 1752-1763" for the many imports by Jesse Fish.

[230] Governor James Grant to "My Lords," November 22, 1764, PRO, CO 5/540, p. 229, from a transcript in the files of the St. Augustine Historical Society Library.

[231] NA. New Orleans Inward Slave Manifests, RG 36, M686, Roll 2.

[232] Slave Database, www.afrigeneas.com.

[233] Charles Johnson, Patricia Smith, WGBH Series Research Team, *Africans in America, America's Journey through Slavery* (1998), pp. 216-217.

[234] *The Georgian*, November 1, 1821, quoting the *Southern Patriot*.

[235] *The Georgian*, November 2, 1821.

[236] *The Georgian*, November 5, 1821.

[237] The libel of the *Hiram* dated Nov. 6, 1821 has the name of the captain, John White. The *Georgian* of November 5 has the names of Robert Wessels and Jack White. A. I. Bulloch in behalf &c vs. Smack Sloop *Hiram* & cargo (included with the libel, NA, Southeast Division)

215

has the names and signatures of the Latin pirates and they are given again with some variation in *The Georgian* of Nov. 5, 1821.

[238] *The Georgian*, November 5, 1821. Lee is further identified in Peter Stephen Chazotte to Capt. Bell, August 18, 1821 (written "within Cape Florida"), NA, Records of the Office of the Secretary of War, RG 107.

[239] *The Georgian*, November 1, 1821.

[240] NA. RG 36, M686, Roll 2.

[241] Gail Swanson, "In Desperation: Indians and Negroes to the Bahamas via Tavernier" *History Talk from the Upper Florida Keys*, Issue 14, Winter, 2000/01; Gail Swanson, "More on the Seminole Negroes' Migration to the Bahamas" *History Talk from the Upper Florida Keys*, Issue 16, Summer, 2001; and Gail Swanson, "Names of Seminole Negroes who fled Florida for the Bahamas via Biscayne Bay & Tavernier Key" *History Talk from the Upper Florida Keys*, Issue 23, Spring, 2003.

[242] May 1 and May 4, 1822 *Royal Gazette* (Bahamas), from notes by John Viele; Carter, *The Territorial Papers of the United States, Florida*, p. 405.

[243] For these ships at Africa see Thomas, p. 616, and see an early copy of my database of the Keys, 1818-1829 at the Monroe County Public Library at Key West.

[244] M. Morgan, M.D., "An account of the Fever that prevailed in the American Squadron, and at Thompson's Island [Key West], 1823," *Philadelphia Journal of Medicine and Philadelphia Science*, Vol. VII, 1824.

[245] NA, Northeast Division. American Insurance Co. & Others vs. Charles Johnson, M919, roll 26 (under the name of the vessel, the *Hercules*).

[246] *The Georgian*, December 18, 1826. I searched NA, Inward Slave Manifests for New Orleans, RG 36.

[247] Census taken by Customs Collector. Island of Key West, 25 Feb., 1828 in "Notes of Early Building in Key West," (paper), State and Local History Room, Monroe County Public Library at Key West.

[248] NA. Log of the *Grampus*; *The Georgian*, July 3, 1830, *Pensacola Gazette*, July 10, 1830 and July 17, 1830; *The African Repository*, vol. VI. The slaver is often refered to by the English translation of the name, the "*Phoenix*."

[249] NA. Supreme Court Case Papers: US v. Schooner *Feniz*, Sept., 1831, in 230/1/33/2, Box 4.

[250] Diary entry May 9, 1831 by Key West resident William Hackley, who boarded the brig. Local and State History Collection, Monroe County Public Library at Key West.

[251] Hackley's diary entry for May 10, 1831.

[252] *The Georgian*, June 22, 1833, summarized by John Viele, "Cholera attack at Key West supposedly brought by brig from New Orleans to Liberia with 120 blacks on board of which 30 or 40 died"; "Letters from Liberia to Kentucky" www.uky.edu/LCC/HIS/scraps/liberia.html (Key West is referred to as a "West Indian Island"); American Colonization Society, Eighteenth Annual Report, Treasurer's Report (1834); "Roll of Emigrants that have been sent to the Colony of Liberia, Western Africa, by the American Colonization Society and its Auxiliaries, to September, 1843, Brig *Ajax*'s Company, arrived at Monrovia July 11, 1833," Christine's Genealogy Website, Freedmen's Bureau Online.

[253] John T. Sprague, *The Florida War* (1964), p. 220.

[254] Robert Schomburgk, *History of Barbados* (1848), p. 436, 442, 443, 449. Betty Shannon at the Barbados Museum & Historical Society sent copies of these pages of this book to me, for which I am grateful.

[255] Historical Records Survey, *Spanish Land Grants*, vol. 3, p. 226.

[256] Historical Records Survey, *Spanish Land Grants*, vol. 1, p 166-167.

[257] *Key West Inquirer*.

[258] *Report of Mr. Kennedy, of Maryland...*, p. 40.

[259] Philip D. Curtin, *The Atlantic Slave Trade, A Census* (1969), p. 188.

[260] Dr. Chukwarah Emeagwali, "The Lost Igbo," www.osondu.com/articles/lostigbo.htm.

[261] Clegg.

[262] Thomas, p. 594

[263] PRO. ADM 37/8414.

[264] The letter was dated "Off Sierra Leone, April 10, 1820" and is printed in *Report of Mr. Kennedy, of Maryland...* p. 297.

[265] PRO. ADM 37/8414.

[266] *The American and Commercial Daily Advertiser* (Baltimore), Jan. 18, 1828.

[267] Letter to the editor of *The American and Commercial Daily Advertiser* from Key West, Dec. 26, 1827, correspondent's name not noted,

published Jan. 14, 1828.

[268] NA. Protest against the brig *Guerrero* by Charles Grover, Joseph Bethel and John Cargo, at Key West, December 26, 1827. RG 59, M179, Roll 66.

[269] PRO. Deposition of Charles Grover, FO 5/236, folio 213.

[270] A letter to the editor of *The American and Commercial Daily Advertiser* from Key West, Dec. 26, 1827, correspondent's name not noted, published Jan. 14, 1828, reads, "The British schooner succeeded in securing 122 slaves, - (1 since dead)." This number seems to be incorrect, as well as the ship they were boarded on, for in his deposition given January 7th Sanderson said, "commenced taking on negroes and received 121 which was the balance left on board." See also letter from Key West, correspondent's name not noted, written Jan. 7, 1828 and extracted in the *Charleston Mercury* of Jan. 16, 1828 which reads, "121 were brought here." But at the risk of not including a life lost I have kept the number "122" rather than "121."

[271] *American and Commercial Daily Advertiser* (Baltimore), Jan. 14, 1828.

[272] This is determined as follows: 121 were brought to Key West and 114 were listed on the manifest of the *General Geddes* bound from Key West to St. Augustine. NA, Document No. 262, Papers relating to the introduction of slaves into the port of St. Augustine, via historian Jerry Wilkinson. The difference is 7. However, Waters Smith states in his April 2, 1828 letter to Representative Joseph M. White, written at St. Augustine: "Six have died since they were landed in Florida." NA, RG 45, 124, Roll 114, p. 16. The difference must be the African that Capt. Doane kept with him. Doane accompanied the *General Geddes* but must have arranged this in Key West and therefore that African was not listed on the manifest.

[273] NA. Waters Smith to Secretary of the Navy John Branch dated at Fernandina, Amelia Island, Florida, August 21, 1829, Misc. Letters Rec'd by the Secretary of the Navy, RG 45, M124, Roll 120.

[274] NA. "Statement showing the present situation of the Africans" in Waters Smith to Samuel L. Southard, dated at Washington City, Oct. 27, 1828, Misc. Letters Rec'd by the Secretary of the Navy, RG 45, M124.

[275] "Statement showing the present situation of the Africans."

[276] NA. Waters Smith to John Branch dated at Fernandina, Amelia Island, Florida, Aug. 21, 1829., RG 124, Misc. Letters Rec'd by the Secretary of the Navy. RG 45. M124.

[277] NA. John Branch to Waters Smith, Sept. 13, 1830, Misc. Letters Sent by the Secretary of the Navy.

[278] NA. John Branch to Waters Smith, Sept. 13, 1830, Misc. Letters Sent by the Secretary of the Navy.

[279] *The African Repository and Colonial Journal*, v. 6 (1830) quoting a letter dated at Liberia, March 20, 1830, correspondent's name not noted.

[280] NA. John Branch to H. McCulloh Jr., Collector, Baltimore, August 14, 1829, Misc. Letters Sent by the Secretary of the Navy.

[281] *The African Repository and Colonial Journal*, v. 6 (1830) quoting a letter dated at Liberia, March 20, 1830, correspondent's name not noted.

[282] NA. A. H. Mechlin to His Excellency James Lyon dated at Carlisle Bay, Barbados, Dec. 21, 1829 (should read Dec. 31), "The American schooner *Washington's Barge* arrived in this port on the 27th inst. having on board ninety-five recaptured Africans," Misc. Letters Rec'd by the Secretary of the Navy, RG 45, and same packet of correspondence, the marine survey, "We the subscribers did repair on board the American schooner *Washington's Barge* A. H. Wing master from Amelia Island for Liberia in Africa having on board one hundred and one liberated Africans and Kroomen." The six Kroomen and the 95 recaptive Africans add up to 101.

[283] *The African Repository and Colonial Journal*, v. 6 (1830) quoting a letter dated at Liberia, March 20, 1830, correspondent's name not noted.

[284] NA. John Boyle, Acting Secretary of the Navy to Reverend R. R. Gurley, American Colonization Society, May 13, 1831; John Boyle to Reverend James Laurie, Colonization Society, May 19, 1831 and Levi Woodburn (?), Navy Department to Reverend R. R. Gurley, June 24, 1831. Misc. Letters Sent by the Secretary of the Navy.

Index

Abbreviation: List: Refers to the list of Africans of the
Guerrero who arrived in Liberia

Adams, John Quincy. 16, 52-54, 66-68, 70, 73, 75, 161
Adele, 152
African Chiefs, 6
African Interpreter, 59-60, 65, 68-69
African Wars, 5, 6
Ajax, 160
Alabama, USS, 157
Alligator, USS, 158
Allison, Thomas, Nimble's Bounty List, pp. 192-194
Amelia Island (see also Fernandina), 74-77, 109
American Colonization Society, 54-55, 70-71, 74, 101, 109
Amistad, 68, 141
Anderson, William, Nimble's Bounty List, pp. 192-194
Antelope, 109, 177-178
Aphrom, Duke, 8
Arcuntasa, Manuel, Guerrero Crew List, pp. 195-196
Ashford, William, Nimble's Bounty List, pp. 192-194
Ashton, Henry, 101
Audubon, John James, 57
Bahamas, 4, 12
Baird, Hugh, Nimble's Bounty List, pp. 192-194
Barbados, 94-100
Barber, 5-6
Barron, James, 81
Barry, Thomas, Nimble's Bounty List, pp. 192-194
Bartow, George, List
Bartow, Joseph, List
Baslida, Isidre, Guerrero Crew List, pp. 195-196
Bason Bank, 143

Beath, Andrew, Nimble's Bounty List, pp. 192-194
Bell, Thomas, 114
Benites, C. A., Guerrero Crew List, pp. 195-196
Berrien, John MacPherson, 129-130
Bethel, Joseph, 24, 29, 130, 162
Bille, Juan, Guerrero Crew List, pp. 195-196
Bing's Landing Preserve, 62
Black Caesar's Creek, 18, 141-143, 146
Blair, Samuel, 102-104
Blair, Selina, 103
Bolivar, 131
Bolton, Charles, 131
Bonner, Thomas, Nimble's Bounty List, pp. 192-194
Bonny River, 7
Bounty, 42, 58-59, 123, 127
Boyle, John, 101
Branch, John, 72-74, 77, 79, 101, 129-130, 162-163
Brent, Daniel, 70
Bridge, Horatio, 121
Brown, Andrew, List
Brown, John, Nimble's Bounty List, pp. 192-194
Brown, Joseph, List
Browne, Fielding A., 42-44, 124, 151, 163
Buchanan, Thomas H., 116-117
Bunce & Disney, 36-37
Bushrod Island, Liberia, 106-108
Cabado, Lucas, Guerrero Crew List, pp. 195-196
Cable, William, Nimble's Bounty List, pp. 192-194
Caesar, see Carysfort Reef Lightship
Caesar, Samson, 114
Calo, Benito, Guerrero Crew List, pp. 195-196
Cambreleng, Churchill, 152
Canning, George, 2
Cape Mesurado, see Liberia
Capetown, Liberia, 117, 121
Capital, 29, 32, 42, 51
Cargo, John, 27

Carter, James, Nimble's Bounty List, pp. 192-194
Carysfort Reef Lightship *Caesar*, 14, 16, 49, 143-146
Cavan, Michael, 99-100
Charleston, S. C., 50-51
Churchward, Richard, 74, 80, 99
Clark, James, List
Clark, Thomas, List
Clark, William, Nimble's Bounty List, pp. 192-194
Clay, Henry, 42, 51-55, 123, 126, 163-164
Clift, Hiram, 151
Cohen, Myer M., 63
Cole, Capt., 100
Congo people, 113, 115-117, 177-179
Conneau, Theophilus, 24
Copp, Belton A., 75
Cornell, Thomas F., 57-58
Cosmopolite, 155-157, 164
Craven, Lieut. T. Augustus, 10
Crespo, Raymond or Ramon, 156
Crusader, USS, 9
Cuban Government Officials, 2, 24-26 (See also Francisco
        Dionisio Vives)
Curtis, John, List
Dana, Joseph, List
Danney, William, Nimble's Bounty List, pp. 192-194
Davis, "Brother," 118-119
Davis, Charles, List
Davis, David, List
Davis, Henry, List
Davis, Isaac, List
Davis, John, List
Davis, July, List
Davis, Lewis, 120
Davis, Louisa, 121
Davis, Thomas, List
Davis, William, Nimble's Bounty List, pp. 192-194
Dawn, Friday, List

Dawn, Sampson, List
Day, John, Nimble's Bounty List, pp. 192-194
Dean, William, Nimble's Bounty List, pp. 192-194
Devany, Henry, List
Devany, James, List
Devany, Samuel, List
Dey (Dei) Tribe, 110-112
Disease, 43-44, 77, 81, 101
Disosway, G. P., 114
Doane, Josiah, 43, 45, 77, 79, 102
Dodd, John P., Nimble's Bounty List, pp. 192-194
Dorsey, Clement, 71
Douglas, Thomas, 58, 103-104
Dozier, Munday, List
Dunlivy, Hugh, Nimble's Bounty List, pp. 192-194
Eboe people, 113, 115-117, 178-179
Eden, James, 113
Edmonston, Charles, 50, 123, 126, 164
Edwards, William, 151
Elliot, Robert H., 21, Nimble's Bounty List, pp. 192-194
Elvira, 101
Emancipados, 41
Enterprise, 160
Ephraim, Duke, 8
Errero, Alexandro, Guerrero Crew List, pp. 195-196
Feniz, 159-160
Fernandes, Antonio, Guerrero Crew List, pp. 195-196
Fernandez, John, List
Fernandina, Florida, 74-81
Fitch, Daniel, 183
Fitzpatrick, Richard, 144, 151, 160
Fleming, Charles E., 40, 56, 123
Florida, 20-21, 26-28, 32, 41, 51
Florida Reef, 18
Flotard, Theo, 63
Forbes, James, 76
Fort George Island, 60

223

Fort San Carlos, 76
Fortinates, Andreo, Guerrero Crew List, pp. 195-196
Franklin, Lt., 159
Gallant, 151
Gallinas River, Africa, 132-138
Gallito, 131
Gallo, 2
Gardener, John, Nimble's Bounty List, pp. 192-194
Garrah tribe, 111
Garretson, H. V., 114
Gawulun, 106
Geddes, John, 50, 123, 149, 164-166
Geddes, George Washington, 50
General Geddes, 29, 32, 50, 51, 57
Gen. Lafayette, 152
General M'Donald, 152
George, Lewis, List
George, Richard, List
Gibbs, Joseph, List
Glover, Nathaniel, 18, 23, 29, 142
Gomez, Joze, 2, 18, 20, 26-27, 46
Gonzales, Antonio, Guerrero Crew List, pp. 195-196
Gonzales, Ramon, 2
Gordon, John, 154-155
Gorman, John, 27
Gould, John, List
Governor Strong, 158
Grampus, USS, 7, 129, 159
Greene, Pardon C., 44, 50, 151
Greenwater, John, Nimble's Bounty List, pp. 192-194
Grover, Charles, 18-23, 27, 142
Guerrero and crewmen, 2, 4, 8, 12-16, 25, 31, 46, 48-49, 52,
    130
Gurley, R. R., 101
Hall, James, 132
Hanson, Captain, List
Hanson, Chap, List

Hanson, John, List
Hanson, John, 70
Hanson, Peter, List
Harper, Samuel H., 159
Havana, Cuba, 2-4, 27, 41, 46, 48, 60, 130-131, 192, 195
Hawkins, William, Nimble's Bounty List, pp. 192-194
Henry, William, Nimble's Bounty List, pp. 192-194
Hercules, 149-151, 158
Hernandez, Joseph M., 60-64, 166
Heroine, 99-100
Herot, R., 184
Higgs Beach, Key West, 45
Hill, Martha, 120
Hiram, 156
Holland, Edward, 4, 19, 21-22, 29, 31, 34-40, 46-48, 50, 52-54, 123-127, 130, 149, 167
Huld, John, Nimble's Bounty List, pp. 192-194
Igbo people, see Eboe people
Indagodora, 2
Indian people, 62, 157
Jackson, Francis, List
Jacksonville, Florida, 69
Jamaica, 40, 48
James, Levi, 157
John Adams, USS, 158
John, List, 101-102
John, Richard, List
Johnson, Charles M., 149, 153, 158
Johnson, John, 150
Jones, John, Nimble's Bounty List, pp. 192-194
Jones, Morice, List
Kai Pa, 112
Kastell, John, Nimble's Bounty List, pp. 192-194
Key West, 17, 30-38, 40, 50, 53-54, 56, 59, 62, 65, 67, 71, 105, 149-160
Kilbee, Henry Theo, 2, 3, 4, 7, 46, 124
Kimmings, Edward, Nimble's Bounty List, pp. 192-194

225

King, George, Nimble's Bounty List, pp. 192-194
Kingsbury, Acey, 27
Kingsley Plantation, 60, 120, 131
Kingsley, Zephaniah, 60, 77-79, 82, 167-168
Kinsley, Adam, List
Kinsley, David, List
Kinsley, Henry, List, 120
Kinsley, James, List, 120
Kinsley, John, 121
Kinsley, Josiah, 120
Kinsley, Louisa, 120
Kinsley, Loumon, List
Kinsley, Lucy, 121
Kinsley, Marshall, List
Kinsley, Monday, 120
Kinsley, Moses, List
Kinsley, Peter, List
Kinsley, Samuel, 121
Kinsley, Sarah, 121
Kinsley, Thomas, List
Kinsley, Thomas, 120
Kinsley, William, List, 121
Kinsley, William, 121
Kinsley, York, List
Kissey, George, List
Kremlin, 159
Kroomen (Kru Tribe), 74, 81, 107, 137
Lacirix, Francisco, Guerrero Crew List, pp. 195-196
Laird, Macgregor, 6
Lambery, 2
Lapwing, 12
Laurie, James, 101
Lee, Judge, 150
Lee, William, 156
Lewis, 59, 68-69
Lewis, America, 120
Lewis, Diana, 120

Lewis, Emanuel, List
Lewis, Fernando, List
Lewis, G. W., Nimble's Bounty List, pp. 192-194
Lewis, John, List
Lewis, Joseph, List
Lewis, Robert, List
Lewis, Sampson, List, 120
Lewis, Samuel, List
Lewis, Thomas, List
Liberia (also referred to as "Cape Mesurado"), 71-74, 94, 96-97, 100-101, 105-122, 138, 177-179, 198
Liberia, 105, 109
Lighthouses, 16, 33
Lilly, 50-51
Lively, 157
Long, Matthew, 63
Loosemore, William, 44-45
Lord, Capt., 153
Lorenzo, Alexandro, Guerrero Crew List, pp. 195-196
Lucas, Jesse, 116
Lucas, Mars, 105, 109, 116
Lyon, James, 94, 99-100, 167-170
Macey, Richard, Nimble's Bounty List, pp. 192-194
Mackay, John, Nimble's Bounty List, pp. 192-194
Macleay, William Sharp, 2, 4, 7, 46, 128
Mala Compra Plantation, 61-63
Manzana, Santiago, 2
March, Philip, Nimble's Bounty List, pp. 192-194
Margy, Juan, 156
Marion, USS, 43, 57, 130, 159
Marshall, Liberia, 118, 121
Martines, Jose, Guerrero Crew List, pp. 195-196
Marvin, William, 19
Mary, 152
Mayo, Isaac, 7
McPhail, John, 73
Mead, Colinette, 121

Mechlin, A. Hamilton, 73-74, 94-97, 99-100
Midas, 10, 130
Migues, John, 156
Millet, Isaac, Nimble's Bounty List, pp. 192-194
Mixed Commission Court, 3, 4, 41, 46, 48
Mohawk, USS, 9
Monkey, HBM, 10, 130-131
Montgomery, Benjamin R., 50
Moore, G., Nimble's Bounty List, pp. 192-194
Moore, John, List
Morgan, Mordecai, 158
Morrison, John, 29-30, 37-38, 50, 58, 123, 124-126, 128,
        144, 170
Murray, George, 141, 147
Murray, John, Nimble's Bounty List, pp. 192-194
Mystic River, Connecticut, 20, 33, 51
Nautilus, 74, 77, 79
Negrito, 131
New Georgia, Liberia, 107-109, 114-121
Newby, James, Nimble's Bounty List, pp. 192-194
Nicholls, Colonel, 6-7
Nigeria area, 5-7, 177
Nimble, HBM, 4, 12-16, 19, 30-32, 37-41, 48-49, 51-52,
        123-127, 130-131
Norfolk, Virginia, 74, 81, 102
North Star, HMS, 10
Nottingham, Henry, Nimble's Bounty List, pp. 192-194
Otero, Jose Axo, Guerrero Crew List, pp. 195-196
Packer, Austin, 20, 27, 51, 128, 171
Parages, Jose C., Guerrero Crew List, pp. 195-196
Paul, Augustus, List
Paul, Henry, List
Paul, John, List
Paul, Samuel, List
Peat, John, Nimble's Bounty List, pp. 192-194
Pelina, Fillio, Guerrero Crew List, pp. 195-196
Pellicer, James, 63

Pensa (Pessa) people, 113, 178
Perry, Matthew C., 158
Pinkney, William, 33-35, 42-43, 45, 52, 56, 59, 65, 128, 171
Pinner, J., Nimble's Bounty List, pp. 192-194
Pinney, Mr., 114
Piracy and the Slave Trade, 2, 7, 8
Prieto, Rafael, Guerrero Crew List, pp. 195-196
Pringle, James, Nimble's Bounty List, pp. 192-194
Ramsey, John, 101
Randall, Richard, 72
Reuben Ross, 12, 183
Revell, John, Nimble's Bounty List, pp. 192-194
Robinson, James, Nimble's Bounty List, pp. 192-194
Rock, Thomas, Nimble's Bounty List, pp. 192-194
Romero, John, 156
Rooke, Thomas, 28
Ropes, William, 74
Ross, Francis James, 69, 77, 172
Rush, Richard, 33, 42, 52-53, 67-68, 172-173
Russel, Alfred Francis, 160
Russwurm, Caesar, List
Russwurm, John B., 116
Ruy, Manuel, Guerrero Crew List, pp. 195-196
Ruys, Raphael, Guerrero Crew List, pp. 195-196
St. Augustine, 42, 45, 57, 60, 67, 80, 101
Salas, Juan Pablo, 50, 149
Salduondo, Pedro Antonio, 2
Salt Bushes Key, 156
San Joze, 2, 25
Sanchez, Venancio, 63
Sand Key, 156
Sanderson, Samuel, 18-19, 22, 46, 51, 127-129, 173
Santa Cruz, Cuba, 21, 24, 26-27, 41
Saunderson, Samuel (See Samuel Sanderson)
Sawyer, John, 51
Scott, Henry, Nimble's Bounty List, pp. 192-194
Seaman, Walter, 150-151

Shark, USS, 158
Sherer, Joseph, 131
Silliman, Joseph A., 155-157
Simmonds, John, Nimble's Bounty List, pp. 192-194
Simonton, John, 149, 151
Slave ship conditions, 8-11
Smith, Adam, List
Smith, Alexander, List
Smith, Anthony, List, 119
Smith, Archibald, List
Smith, Cafara, 120
Smith, Caroline, 120
Smith, George, List, 120
Smith, Glasgow, List
Smith, Grudging, List
Smith, James, List
Smith, James, Nimble's Bounty List, pp. 192-194
Smith, Jesse, List
Smith, John, List
Smith, John Vaughn, 73-74, 98
Smith, Joseph, List
Smith, Joseph Lee, 65, 69, 173
Smith, Lamb, List
Smith, Lewis, List
Smith, Major, List
Smith, Margaret, 120
Smith, Mary, 80
Smith, Mary, 120
Smith, Ned, List
Smith, Pedro, List
Smith, Pepper, List
Smith, Peter, 120
Smith, Richard, List
Smith, Robert, List
Smith, Samuel, List
Smith, Thomas, 27
Smith, Thomas, List

Smith, Thomas, 120
Smith, Waters, 42-43, 53, 57-60, 64, 68-73, 77-82, 101-104, 151, 173-174
Smith, William, Nimble's Bounty List, pp. 192-194
Smith, William, 120
Southard, Samuel Lewis, 59, 66, 68-72, 123-127, 174
Stacey, M. H., 9
Stanard, Robert B., 183
Stewart, John, List
Stodgell, William, Nimble's Bounty List, pp. 192-194
Stotesbury, Capt., 79
Strong, John B., 50, 149
Superior, 60
Surprize, 18-19, 27, 29-32, 36, 39, 46, 48, 51
Swanson, Peter, Nimble's Bounty List, pp. 192-194
Tavernier Key, 33, 143, 157
Teague, Mr., 118, 122
Telegraph, 44
Thompson, Lt., 112
Thorn, 18, 20, 22-24, 26-27, 29-30, 32, 36, 41, 46, 128
Tift, Asa C., 50
Tingle, George E., 36, 51
Townsend, John, Nimble's Bounty List, pp. 192-194
Transit, 152
Travis, Cyrus, List
Travis, Philip, List
Trevanion, G. B., Nimble's Bounty List, pp. 192-194
Tucker, Philip, List
Vaughan, Charles, 52-53, 55-56, 123, 175
Veloz, 10
Venus, 160
Vernande, Antonio, Guerrero Crew List, pp. 195-196
Verpup, John, Nimble's Bounty List, pp. 192-194
Vey (Vei) tribe, 107, 110
Vidal, Capt., 6
Virginia, 152
Vives, Francisco Dionisio, 3, 46-48

Walker, John, 32, 42, 51, 130, 175
Walsh, Robert, 10
Walters, Samuel, Nimble's Bounty List, pp. 192-194
Washington Oaks State Gardens, 61-62
Washington's Barge, 74, 80-99
Watson, William, Nimble's Bounty List, pp. 192-194
Wessels, Robert, 156
West, William, 158
Westfall, Henry F., 114
Whalton, John, 14, 20, 22, 51, 128, 143, 176
White, Enrique, 75
White, Jack, 156
White, Joseph M., 69, 72, 104, 127
Whitehead, John, 151
Wildfire, 9-10, 45
Wilkie, Charles G., Nimble's Bounty List, pp. 192-194
William Tell, 74
Williams, Alfred Brockenbrough, 107
Williams, Amy, 120
Williams, Henry, List, 120
Wing, A. H., 74, 80, 95-99
Wirt, William, 66
Woodburn, Levi, 102
Wright, William, 27, 46-47, 128-129